THE BABY MATRIX

Why Freeing Our Minds From Outmoded Thinking About Parenthood & Reproduction Will Create a Better World

LAURA CARROLL

LiveTrue Books, http://livetruebooks.com

ISBN 978-0-615-64299-4

Jacket design by Creativindie Covers

~For Michael~

CONTENTS

INTRODUCTION

Why It's Time for This Manifesto

In the movie *The Matrix*, the character Morpheus offers two pills to Neo—if he takes the blue pill, he will go on with life as he has before, believing what he has always believed. If he takes the red pill, he will find out what the "matrix" really is, and many of his earlier beliefs will be shattered. When it comes to taking a hard look at a specific set of beliefs that has driven our society for generations, *The Baby Matrix* is the red pill. It unravels these beliefs and shows us why they no longer serve us—or why they were never true in the first place.

What is this set of beliefs? It's called "pronatalism," meaning "pro"-"natal" or "pro-baby." It's the idea that parenthood and raising children should be the central focus of every person's adult life. Pronatalism is a strong social force and includes a collection of beliefs so embedded that they have come to be seen as "true."

For some people, perhaps you, there may be nothing more fulfilling than raising a child. But I think you'd agree that parenthood is not automatically the right choice for everyone. You don't have to look very far to find parents who never should have had children.

The problem with pronatalism is that it leads *everyone* to believe they should have children—even people who shouldn't have children. And pronatalism leads people to believe they have the right to have as many children as they want—even people who shouldn't have children. This creates problems that extend beyond families and the children who may be suffering from the effects of poor parenting. At a time when we humans are consuming resources over 50 percent faster than the planet is producing them, every choice to bear a child has implications for the larger community. That's why this conversation about pronatalism is one that involves all of us, parents or not.

During my research for *Families of Two* and since then, I have learned a lot about how pronatalist beliefs affect us individually and collectively, and not in a positive way. This has been explored before; in the 1970s, Ellen Peck and Judith Senderowitz confronted pronatalism head-on with *Pronatalism: The Myth of Mom & Apple Pie*. Their book includes chapters with a number of different contributing authors who explain what pronatalism is, how and why it is so pervasive in society, and the negative effects of that pervasiveness.

It's time to take another hard look at pronatalism. Many people have begun to question its tenets, and rightly so. They are waking up to the fact that this set of implicit assumptions furthers the agendas of power structures such as the church, state, and industry—*not* individuals. They are questioning how they've been unconsciously influenced to accept beliefs that ultimately serve others' agendas, and how this negatively impacts not just themselves but people from all walks of life. Pronatalist assumptions dictate how we're supposed to follow the "normal path" to adulthood. They also put unwarranted pressure on us to have biological children (and the "right" number of them), fail to foster a society in which those who are best suited to become parents are the ones who have children, and do a disservice to children who are already here in need of loving homes. The assumptions also result in inequitable workplace and tax policies that favor parents over people with no children. And they work against leaving future generations a better world.

It's time for all of us to understand why we can no longer afford to leave pronatalist assumptions unquestioned and why now is the time to transition to a "post" pronatal society. *The Baby Matrix* is the manifesto to ignite this transition. In this book, I present seven long-held pronatalist assumptions and the reasons they are incorrect, are no longer necessary, or no longer work. I lay out an alternative set of assumptions that reflects present realities and supports true reproductive freedom and reproductive responsibility in today's society.

Don't misunderstand: I am not against people who choose to become parents. *The Baby Matrix* urges all of us to take a closer look at pronatal assumptions in order to see the truth about parenthood, reproduction, and our future. Like the red pill in *The Matrix*, which instigates an awakening to what is real, this book takes a hard look at why it's so important to stop blindly believing pronatalist doctrine and start realizing its serious costs. It poses powerful ways to shift our thinking for the betterment of all.

This book is for anyone who reveres the truth and wants the best for themselves, their families, and our world. If that's you, I say go down the pronatal rabbit hole where you will find the truths that need to be told, and see why I invite you to join me in being part of the emergence of a post-pronatal society.

1

AWAKENING TO PRONATALISM

Grist.org, a well-known environmental news and commentary site, claimed that 2010 was the year that "childless by choice" or the "childfree" went "mainstream."[1] However, mainstream it isn't. Having children remains the norm. If having no children by choice was part of the norm, it would mean that those who make this choice would be members of a widely-accepted group and that we as a society have accepted their choice. This is not the case. Why does our society find this choice so hard to accept? It boils down to an old and dominant underlying social force in our country called pronatalism.

What is Pronatalism?

Pronatalism is a powerful ideology and set of beliefs that goes back many generations. The book, *Pronatalism: The Myth of Mom & Apple Pie*, gives one of the best definitions of pronatalism: "... an attitude or policy that is pro-birth, that encourages reproduction, that exalts the role of parenthood."[2] With its definition comes a host of supporting societal assumptions that might have served a purpose at one time, but have now outlasted their usefulness, or have actually never been true at all.

At its core, pronatalism is designed to glorify parenthood. While the existence of this glorification has a long history, in her 1995 book,

Why Don't You Have Kids?, author Leslie Lafayette wrote that the 90s may have been "the most pronatalistic period of our society."[3] However, it can be argued that the most pronatalistic time in our society is *now*. As Ellen Walker comments in *Complete Without Kids*, we are living in a time of "baby worship."[4] Thanks to celebrities and the media, pregnancy and the raising of children is glamorized like no other time in history.

While pronatalism is everywhere and affects all of us, it has not been seriously examined as a driving force in our society today. As far back as 1974, Peck contended that pronatalism was not talked about enough because it's one of modern society's "invisible devices." That is to mean, then and now, it's so pervasive that we no longer realize it's there.[5] To understand this pervasiveness, let me take you back in time to its origins and what led to the numerous ways its power manifests in so many areas of our lives.

Where Did Pronatalism Come From?

Historically, pronatalistic values have been driven by two motives: survival and power. Throughout human history, valuing fertility was necessary to ensure survival. For example, to ensure population growth in Roman times, ruler Caesar Augustus instituted the Augustan Laws, which rewarded people who had many children and penalized childlessness.[6] The laws promoted the idea that it was a person's duty to ensure the survival of its society.

From as far back as 50 BC, the Fathers of the Christian Church instilled the idea of duty as well. It was a person's duty to God to "be fruitful and multiply." Idolizing the role of motherhood ensured a growing population of the church's members, which would continue to increase the church's religious power. Over many years in history, the church's pronatalist forces have reigned along with social and political forces as societies developed. Encouraging and even mandating population growth was important to offset population losses due to infant mortality, war, and disease. And the larger a society's population, the more it could expand and gain power.

High fertility has been necessary in any time of settlement in new territory. For early American settlers, for example, children were necessary for survival. Children, and lots of them, were needed to work the land and help with all that comes with homesteading. During this time, says sociologist E.E. LeMasters, people had children with no "great expectation," other than "simple care, nurture, and teaching of rural settlement skills." Having children was a practical matter, and one that brought economic benefit to a family.[7]

However, women's valued reproductive role didn't come without its downsides and risks. LeMasters pointed out that when a social role such as motherhood and fatherhood is difficult, a romantic myth needs to surround it to keep it in its most positive light.[8] In this case, idealizing pregnancy and motherhood would continue to guarantee women would have children and ensure survival. Early feminist Leta Hollingsworth wrote of the sources of these myths, or "social devices" as she called them, that were needed to emphasize the positives of parenthood and encourage pregnancy. In her 1916 paper, "Social Devices for Impelling Women to Bear and Raise Children," Hollingsworth laid out nine social devices or forms of social control that promote the perpetuation of pronatalism.[9]

She called the first social device the creation of certain "personal ideals" of what it means to be a "normal" woman. These include pushing ideas like the belief that a "womanly woman" means wanting to be a mother, and wanting children is just part of being a woman. To admit otherwise would make one appear abnormal, something no one wanted to be. Hollingsworth also spoke of the social device she called "public opinion." This device was found in all the different types of media at that time, such as newspapers and magazines. Another social device that reinforced natalism was the law, such as laws that rewarded births and outlawed birth control and abortion. Laws preventing women from owning property were particularly powerful in fortifying natalism; not being able to own property of their own made women more dependent on men to provide them the place to do what socially accepted, womanly women did—have children.

Hollingsworth also spoke to "belief" as a social device—specifically, those religious in nature. This includes any messages that promote reproduction as one's duty to God. Education was another social device that was designed to ingrain early in students' minds the idea that they are destined to grow up and become parents. Art was another powerful social device that upheld the ideal of motherhood, from painting to literary works and song.

"Illusion" has also served as a social device. Those who perpetuated illusions made sure that pregnancy and child rearing were spoken of in positive terms only, and they made it taboo to talk about the negatives, such as the agonies that can be present at childbirth, the tragedy of the death of the mother and/or the baby in childbirth, or the drudgery and challenges of raising children. They magnified the joys of motherhood so that women believed the illusions rather than recognized the realities.

Last, Hollingsworth talked about the social device, "bugaboos." These are supposed facts to influence women to have babies. For example, at the time she wrote this paper, to encourage women to have babies early in life, doctors told women that if they delayed pregnancy until 30 years or older, the "pains and dangers will be gravely increased." The medical community at the time also purported that women who bore children would live longer than women who didn't, and there were serious perils associated with having only one child.

These kinds of social devices have been the means by which pronatalism became a powerful social influence in society. They supported the post-World War II baby boom, along with the idealization of domestic life during that time, as men came home from the war and women returned home from men's jobs they had taken while the men were gone. These social devices continued and remained intact even during the women's movement. While the movement empowered women in a number of ways, it did not challenge childbearing directly. The empowerment that came from access to birth control focused more on their power to choose *when* to have a child, not *whether* to have a child at all.

Since the time of the women's movement, these kinds of expectations and pressures on women to become mothers have remained strong. When women began having careers outside the home, they began delaying parenthood, which fueled an increase in the numbers of women having infertility treatments. And while the 2008 U.S. Census fertility report tells us that peak childbearing years are between 25-29, the infertility business is going strong, as more women than ever over 40 years old are having their first child. According to the National Center for Health Statistics, between 1980 and 2004, the number of women giving birth at age 30 doubled, it tripled at age 35, and almost quadrupled after age 40. Birth rates are lower today than 30 years ago; the 2008 Census report indicates that women aged 40-44 had an average of 1.9 children compared to 3.1 in 1976. People may be having fewer children later these days, but it remains a social given that they will have them.[10]

Just like in times past, media, law, religion, education, and art support pronatalist ideals. Even today, there are taboos about telling the entire truth about parenthood, and the medical community also provides questionable information. Today, as in the past, social forces are reinforcing the universal idealization of parenthood and maternity.

Why Does Pronatalism Remain Pervasive Today?

You might ask yourself why pronatalism remains rampant today when we don't have the "underpopulation" worries of societies past. Even though we theoretically no longer need the social control mechanisms because population shortage is certainly not a problem, these social controls have hammered the universal longing for motherhood into our cultural hardware so hard for so long that it has sunk deeply into the fabric of our consciousness, culture, beliefs, and values. In a word, pronatalism is the norm. Like with other norms, we learn early in life what is expected, what the "rules" are, and why they are "right." Being around others conforming to the norms constantly reinforces those beliefs and influences our behavior.

Social controls are still in place for survival and power. Today, three realms greatly benefit from the perpetuation of pronatalism. Keeping pronatalism alive guarantees that government, the church, and businesses will continue to flourish and gain power. Government wants to encourage births so tax bases will grow, which ensures its survival and continued power. The church wants its adherents to cherish childbirth and parenthood so that the church can continue to gain more followers, which ensures its survival and continued power. More than ever today, business reaps the rewards of a pro-baby, pro-parenthood society because it supports the growth of capitalism. Pushing pro-baby values because of the demand it creates for products and services brings big profits to business. These power realms work to keep pronatalist norms in place and promote reproductive conformity.

The Media

The power of pronatalism in business is very evident in all forms of media. And it's so rampant that so much of the time, we don't even notice it. Studies since the 1940s have shown that magazines come from a strong pronatalist position. Articles and advertisements project the ideal woman as mother, while glorifying pregnancy, babies, and raising children. Visual messages reinforce the awe and glorification of motherhood. Childbearing celebrities have never been more popular. Magazines idolize parenthood through the lives of the stars; in articles and photos, they follow the rich and famous' every natal move. In other print media, such as newspapers, we see countless articles and ads portraying the happy and amazing lives of families with children.

It's all over digital media as well, from ezines to the deluge of parenthood and parenting sites, not to mention digital advertising. Even the tech culture is child-centric in its approaches to advertising. Websites that have nothing to do with pregnancy, parenthood, or kids have Google ads about all of these things. Why? The algorithms pick up on certain words and associate them with their pronatalist roots. Or take Facebook—why do we see pregnancy ads on a 20-something's page on her birthday? The algorithm must predict that she will be getting pregnant soon. It seems the algorithms take certain facts or words from the site and formulate associations from a larger cultural context, not the context in which it appears. And that cultural context is child-centric.

Advertising on television, in print, and in digital media use pregnancy as a product sales tool. We see sentimentalized images of children and a multitude of products solving parents' problems. Pregnancy-related and children's products are big business. Advertising even uses the image of "family" to sell its products, whether the product is designed for that purpose or not.

Where else but in a child-centric society would television shows featuring a "mega-family" become a reality show sensation? These shows—"19 Kids and Counting" featuring the Duggars, "Kate Plus," "Rising Sextuplets," and "Table for 12"—all celebrate the idea that you can never have too many children. And of course, there's the media sensation, Nadya Suleman or the "Octomom," who has a television documentary about her family of fifteen.

On the opposite side, it's often what we don't see that points more powerfully to pronatalism at work. How often do we see shows where there are couples without children because they are happy that way? Or dialogue that makes it clear that this is the case and an integral part of the show's story? On talk shows, print media, and digital media, how often do you hear from celebrities about the *joys* of being a celebrity with no children? In the last few years, some celebrities have spoken out a bit more about their childfree status, but it's nothing compared to the attention that celebrity parents get. Instead, from all media directions, we get sent the message that "family," meaning parenthood and children, is what's in style.

Baby as Status Accessory

Celebrities, coupled with our status-driven culture, have taken the baby-craze to new heights. People watch celebrities have perfect pregnancies and the "supernova" version of parenthood they present. They have wealth, the perfect family, and all the parenting accoutrements that show their socioeconomic status. They have the nannies and fandango strollers. Their children go to all the right private schools, starting with hard-to-get-into pre-schools. Like the best Prada bag, their number of homes, and their glamorous lifestyles, their perfect children help show the world that they are at the top of the success heap.

According to *Momzillas* author, Jill Kargmen, the baby-as-accessory concept has morphed "into the idea that one isn't enough. It manifests in the status symbol of four-is-the-new-three megafamilies in New York, where just by having that many kids, it's like saying we have Oprah money; we can hack four tuitions, five bedrooms, the help, the life."[11] The number of children it appears you can afford to have reflects your socioeconomic status in life, and like money, more is better.

People are motivated to emulate this picture of perfection, and not just in the upper socioeconomic echelons. An inordinate amount of energy goes into being perfect parents today. Jennifer Senior, a *New York Times* journalist who has written on the lives of parents, describes this energy as the "aggressive cultivation" that parents put into their kids these days. They want to be perfect parents of perfect kids.[12] This phenomenon has taken the pronatalist norm to new heights and helps keep it even more pervasive, because now more than ever before, parents can use their children as a tool for status achievement and recognition.

Policy

Governmental policy, particularly in the area of tax law, operates as a social control to reward reproduction. There are a number of ways the tax code benefits parents. For example, there is a personal exemption for each child under 19, or under 24 if the son/daughter is a full-time student. If the parents are divorced, the exemption goes to the parent who had most of the custody of the child. There is also the "child credit" or a tax reduction per child, as well as a "child care tax credit" and income tax credits for parents. Other examples include how parents have the opportunity to contribute to educational savings accounts with tax-free withdrawals for education-related expenses and get tax breaks from tuition programs in the form of higher education tuition credits and deductions.

Programs like welfare are intended to help those with little or no income, and this is a good thing. However, they are structured such that the welfare payments rise with the birth of the first child and rise again with each additional child. This not only encourages births, but does so for women who can't afford it. Because of the demands of childcare, having more children can make it even more difficult for a mother to find work and break the cycle that keeps her on welfare.

Local laws also favor parents and children. For example, local property taxes very often go to public schools. Those with no children don't pay less than those with children, and depending on their reported income, they can easily pay more than families with children. Those with no children pay into the school system to invest in the country's future, but parents see the more direct benefit and more value for their tax dollars.

State, federal, and corporate policies also encourage pregnancy through parental leave policies. This kind of policy has its benefits. A recent report by the Center for Economic and Policy Research indicates that over 90 percent of employees who used paid parental leave (with partial wage replacement) said it "had a positive effect on their ability to care for their babies." Employees also reported that it improves a dad's bonding with his newborn. It also indicates that California's program had "no or very little impact on their business operations." In fact, 89 percent surveyed said this kind of leave had either no effect or a positive effect on productivity, 96 percent said it reduced employee turnover, and 99 percent said it improved morale.[13]

According to Jeremy Adam Smith, author of *The Daddy Shift: How Stay-at-Home Dads, Breadwinning Moms, and Shared Parenting Are Transforming the American Family*, only seven percent of men take advantage of parental leave, but about half of America's women have access to it.[14] While parents can take this time to care for their new baby, those with no children (yet or by choice) don't get that time. All of these types of benefits favor and reward those who choose to reproduce, not those who do not.

The Church

The role religious organizations play as a pronatalist force cannot be underestimated. Christianity and Islamic religions are the two largest religions in the world, both of which adulate children and the role of parent. Over 78 percent of Americans are Christian. Most Americans are either Protestant (about 51 percent) or Catholic (24 percent).[15] To one degree or another, Christians believe it is the word of God to propagate, that their children are gifts from God, and that they have a moral duty to bring God's gifts into the world. The Catholic Church believes in procreation so strongly that it forbids the use of birth control as a family planning tool and professes that a woman will die "in sin" if on any kind of birth control at the time of death. Just fewer than two percent of Americans practice Judaism, which also strongly values procreation. Together, most religions play a powerful role in influencing people to have children to fulfill their obligation to their chosen religious communities.

Schools

Pronatalist messaging begins at an early age in schools, from the first time children are told, in one way or another, that one day they, too, will be parents. Parenthood biases promulgate with teachers and textbooks, but these biases have not been studied much. One of the few studies that looked at biases in textbooks was done in the 1970s by Nancy Cox of the State of Maryland Commission on the Status of Women.[16] Cox developed criteria to help identify pronatalism in textbooks and used them to determine whether they had a pronatal bias. The criteria included: 1) When "inevitability of parenthood is assumed," 2) when "childfree lifestyles and/or marriages are not acknowledged," 3) when "childfree marriages are treated as problematic or undesirable," and 4) when there is "adherence to theories of maternal instinct or maternity as central to women's life." Cox surveyed textbooks used in the home economics department in the Baltimore County school system and found most had a pronatal bias.

These criteria can still be used today to evaluate textbooks and the attitudes teachers have that influence their students' thinking on parenthood. But have they been? This area has been sorely understudied. Biases as they relate to how gender roles appear in texts have been studied and show that there has been improvement in this area. Religious bias has also been studied, and, as a result, textbooks have shown more sensitivity in this regard in recent years. This isn't the case for parenthood bias.

The fact that there has been very little research on pronatalistic biases in schools suggests that these exist. Why the lack of study? Because pronatalism is the norm, and the expectation of parenthood is so strong, we just don't think to question it, much less study the impact of its influence.

We also see the evidence of pronatalism in the lack of classroom discussion about the childfree lifestyle choice. Because parenthood is assumed, the childfree lifestyle is rarely talked about in the classroom.

If it is, it likely includes less than positive explanations and stereotypes. Most theories of gender identity still see womanhood as synonymous with motherhood, so students are taught to understand it in this way, which only reinforces the adulation of motherhood and parenthood.

Film, Books, Music, & Art

Pronatalism lives in story, in the form of film, books, and song. So many films feature love and relationships moving ultimately in the direction of marriage and children. In her piece, "Go Forth and Multiply," Eve Kushner, author of *Experiencing Abortion: A Weaving of Women's Words*, accurately and wittily speaks to how pronatalist imperatives show up in films. In her words, some popular messages in films that idolize pregnancy and parenthood include:

❖ If you have an unplanned pregnancy, birth is the only option … even if you or your partner is unhappy about the conception.

❖ If circumstances make the pregnancy problematic, don't worry—everything will work out somehow. Just be happy. After all, a baby is on the way.

❖ You will glow with pride and femininity as you proceed with the noble mission of carrying (the baby) to term.

❖ When you deliver the child, there will again be irrepressible joy and widespread celebration. It'll be glaringly obvious that birth was the only valid decision.

❖ If you're a man, you may feel unready or unwilling to have a baby (but) should rise to the occasion and improve yourself if necessary.

❖ Babies only strengthen romances. Couples may worry that new babies could stress out their relationship. But no—babies keep families together.

❖ What this world needs is babies, babies, babies. Bring them on by the caseload. Don't stop to think about the population explosion. Only sarcastic, recalcitrant jokers and misanthropes would be so low as to point out that three or four children might be more than enough for one couple.

❖ A childless life is worthless, and anyone who doesn't want kids must be bitter and selfish and morally deficient. If you postpone or eschew parenthood, you'll face a future of unhappiness and regret.[17]

In a word, storylines in film tell us that pregnancy and babies will bring the happy ending. On the flipside, pronatalism is reinforced by what we don't see in the movies. While there are childfree singles, we don't see childfree couples living just as fulfilling lives as those who are parents. The film, *Sex and the City 2,* is a rare example. Carrie and John are explicitly content together being childfree, but the storyline can't let that alone; in the film, Carrie has to question whether their life together shouldn't be something more.

In books, it is hard to find fiction that has protagonists who are childfree, much less stories that don't in one way or another cast the childfree in a negative light. As childfree column writer Lori Bradley observes, "Many stories begin with an interesting main character, only to disappoint as the character devolves into an obsession with children or childbearing."[18] In nonfiction, even women's history books often don't acknowledge the existence of the childfree, much less the rising numbers of them. For example, in the recent book, *When Everything Changed: The Amazing Journey of American Women from 1960 to the Present,* respected author and journalist Gail Collins does not touch on the childfree life at all. Instead, she speaks to "the expectation that sooner or later a baby would come" and that in the new millennium, women have not been, "in general, responding to work stress by opting not to have children."[19] She does not mention the rising numbers of women who are opting out of motherhood, or that for women aged 40-44, the numbers have doubled since the

1970s.[20] There are nonfiction works on the childfree life, but they are characteristically written by the childfree themselves, who oftentimes attempt to justify and demystify this lifestyle choice.

In song, we hear pronatalism's presence when the lyrics reinforce the life path—find love, find your life partner, and have children together to experience life's raison d'etre, life's biggest gift of all. We hear it anytime the lyrics exalt the bearing and raising of children and express woes about a life without children. We hear it anytime the lyrics uphold the ideals associated with motherhood and father-hood. You don't have to tune in very closely to find these messages throughout popular music. We are so used to hearing them, we often don't realize they are there.

The same goes for the visual arts. In many historical periods of art, children have been idolized. This goes back to periods long ago in which paintings had religious themes. Today, anytime you see a painting or any visual work that puts mothers, fathers, and children on a pedestal or is designed to instill feelings of admiration for such themes, it invariably arises from the bedrock of pronatalist values in the culture. Just like with music, you don't have to look around much to see pronatalism is all around us in public murals, posters on the side of a bus, or works in art galleries.

Collectively, these cultural expressions keep pronatalism alive and well, but they are not at the root of what truly drives the strength of pronatalism. Underneath these are the core attitudes and beliefs— the value-based *assumptions* of pronatalism. The following chapters examine these assumptions and why we need to let go of them. They propose the adoption of alternative assumptions which reflect today's realities and promote ideas and practice that will make for a better world for all of us.

2

THE DESTINY ASSUMPTION

The first pronatalist assumption that deserves a hard look has to do with our fate in life. Pronatalist dogma tells us that everyone is destined to become parents. Today, because more people are starting to have children later, the assumption could be expanded so say, "We're all supposed to want them—*eventually*." Why? Because we are supposedly hard-wired to have children. Or said another way, the pronatalist assumption has been:

We have a biological instinct to have children.

From an early age, we're taught that we'll grow up and have children one day. Women in particular are given strong messages that they are wired to have children and *want* them. They're told they'll experience this uncontrollable urge from deep within calling them to become mothers and fulfill their biological purpose. Women are led to believe that this urge is primitive and has been hard-wired over many years of evolution. If this primal urge never arises, we're told there must be something wrong with us. Giving birth, we're told, is a basic human need.

Looking Closer

Let's look at the heart of this assumption and ask, what is instinct? When we think of it in relation to animals, we think of behaviors they just "do" without any training. For instance, birds know how to build nests, newborn sea turtles know how to walk into the ocean, and most animals know how to fight and protect themselves. Do human beings have instincts? Psychologists and sociologists have defined instinct differently over time, as research about human behavior has become more rigorous. By the end of the 1800s, these experts considered most kinds of repeated human behaviors as instinctive. By around the 1980s, however, psychologists like Abraham Maslow began to argue that humans have evolved to the point that they're not at the mercy of their instincts. He asserted that "humans no longer have instincts because we have the ability to override them in certain situations." Maslow and many psychologists and sociologists agreed that if we can choose to override a behavior, it isn't an instinct.[1]

Some experts argue that the desire for sex constitutes a biological instinct or primal urge. This may have been true in earlier phases of human evolution, but as humans and societies developed, having sex was not something people just automatically did; they consciously chose to engage in it. Sex and pregnancy are behaviors that, in Maslow's terms, can be "overridden." Seen this way, even sleep and hunger are not human instincts. It may seem extreme to say this, but the truth is we can choose to engage in these behaviors or not.

In addition, there is no real evidence to support the notion that everyone has a "biological instinct for the desire to bear children." In the words of author Ellen Peck, "Conception is biological; pregnancy is biological. Birth is biological. Parenthood is psychological in its application."[2] Just because we humans have the biological ability to conceive and bear children does not mean we have an instinctive desire to become parents or even have the ability *to* parent.

We know that during pregnancy, the woman is under the influence of hormones like estrogen and progesterone, which kick in at conception and continue through pregnancy, along with the neurohormone, oxytocin, which fires at the time of delivery. Research also indicates that biology is at work in mom once the baby is born. For example, a good deal of research tells us that the scent of the baby becomes chemically imprinted in mom within the first few days of the baby's life. Mom's brain also responds differently to various baby behaviors; her brain activity looks different when the baby is smiling versus when it is not smiling.[3]

But what about *before* pregnancy and motherhood begins? What hard-wired biological process *creates* the desire for a child, or what neuropsychiatrist Louann Brizendine calls "baby lust—the deep felt hunger to have a child"? Brizendine contends that certain smells, like the smell of an infant's head, carry pheromones that stimulate a woman's brain to produce "the potent love potion oxytocin—creating a chemical reaction that induces baby lust," that somehow is "nature's sneak attack to trigger the desire to have a baby."[4] If the brain worked in this way to create the longing, the urge, all women would end up feeling this way. But they don't. All women don't experience baby lust—so is it a lack of oxytocin or something else?

Research has looked at other biological processes that somehow get the "biological clock" ticking in women and men. A recent study done by St. Andres and Edinburgh Universities tells us that women lose about 90 percent of their eggs by the age of thirty.[5] So we know there is egg loss, but how is it connected to the "biological urge" that many women claim comes over them? Is it because women are getting down to the final number of eggs, and somehow, their reproductive system instinctively sends their brains a message saying, "Use those eggs now!"? Like the supposed magical flood of oxytocin, if this sort of biological process was truly at work, all women would feel it. As far back as the 1970s, researcher and psychoanalyst Dr. Frederick Wyatt said, "When a woman says with feeling she craved her baby from within, she is putting biological language to what is psychological."[6] Rather than a biological process, it's a psychological process. The woman realizes that her reproductive years are coming to an end and that she might miss out on what pronatalist society tells her is the most fulfilling experience in life. Believing she might not get to have this experience can create quite the yearning for it.

The longing or yearning can also come from a desire to find purpose in life. Rather than delve into and figure out what purpose and fulfillment means to her, strong pronatalist messages make it easy for her to believe that "the" way to find purpose and meaning is through motherhood. Not only is she doing what all women are supposed to do in life, but she is also choosing the socially acceptable path, according to pronatalism.

How does the longing, the urge, work for men? Researchers have looked at how a biological "clock" relates to sperm and age. A good deal of research tells us what happens to men's sperm as they age and how that affects fertility. Dr. Ethylin Jabs, Director of the Center for Craniofacial Development and Disorders at Johns Hopkins, sums up the research by saying that the "bottom line is: As men age, the percentage of damaged sperm they carry in their testes tends to increase."[7] Recent studies from Israel, California, and Sweden have connected "late paternal age" (statistically, "late paternal age" starts at 30) with some serious medical conditions. The longer a man waits to have a child, the more likely his child will be affected by things like schizophrenia, dwarfism, bipolar disorder, or autism. In some cases, the risk factors skyrocket. A 2005 study conducted by the University of California, Los Angeles, found a fourfold rise in Down syndrome among babies born to men 50 and older.[8] In his book, *The Male Biological Clock: The Startling News About Aging, Sexuality, and Fertility in Men,* Harry Fisch addresses similar risks and discusses what happens to men's ability to have children as they get older.[9]

So this tells us that the longer men let their biological clocks tick, the greater the risk of having a baby with a birth defect due to the poor quality of their sperm. But where is the biological link to wanting children to begin with? While many men don't describe the same kind of emotional yearning that women talk about, many feel strongly about wanting to become a father. Why? Because they've bought into the notion that becoming a father means they are virile, and that through fatherhood, they will find the true legacy of their lives.

We can look at the question of whether men or women have a biological instinct to want or have children another way. Rather than biological, the urge, the wanting has its roots in a *learned desire from strong social and cultural pronatal influences.* And we've been influenced so strongly that it feels like the desire for children is "innate"—it's so ingrained that we've thought it's just part of who we are. Lena Hollingsworth gets to the heart of why it isn't: If wanting children was actually an instinct, there would be no need for the social controls to encourage and influence reproduction.[10] If it were truly instinctive, there would be no need for the "social devices" and cultural pressures to have children. If it were instinctive, childbearing rates would remain high. Humans wouldn't think about it; they would just have babies and continue until they biologically could not.

Instead, childbearing numbers have varied over time. For example, in the 1930s, 20 percent of women had no children; in 1970, this number was 12 percent. Since the 1970s, the percentages have almost doubled, and recent figures are at about 20 percent. If it's instinctive to want children, we would not see this variability, nor would we see what the Center for Work Life Policy reports as the "exceptionally large number" of Gen Xers who are choosing not to have children.[11]

For too long, pronatalist propaganda created by social institutions to control human behavior has influenced our emotions, thinking, and social values. It's time to recognize that the pronatal assumption that we are biologically destined to want children is *not* a biological reality. What is the reality?

The Alternative Assumption

Our biological capacities allow us to make parenthood a choice.

At one time, it was necessary to create social mechanisms to promote childbearing and ensure increases in population. The old

Destiny Assumption has been one of those mechanisms. Look at where it's taken us. We now have more people on the planet than generations past could have ever imagined. We no longer need to live by the old notion that biology is destiny in order to ensure our survival. Now, we can hold beliefs that reflect what is real. Our biological reproductive capacity creates the possibility of reproduction, and our biologically-endowed ability to think and feel affords us the capacity to choose when and whether to have children. Social manipulation makes us think otherwise, but reproduction is ultimately a choice; it isn't an instinctual drive.

The Larger Reality

The Alternative Assumption reflects the current truth that we no longer need population growth. The global population is seven billion and counting, so no social good can come from continuing to believe that we're all destined to reproduce. According to Robert Walker, the Executive Vice President of the Population Institute, we could see the population rise by another two billion by mid-century, a calamity in a world already struggling to feed the seven billion plus people who are already here.[12] Given our current population-related problems, we are far better served by a mindset that gives equal legitimacy to becoming a parent or remaining childfree.

Promoting the Right Parenthood Choice

The Alternate Assumption gives us back the power to make parenthood a conscious choice. It opens the way for us to look at whether we want the experience of raising children, and if we think we do, to look harder at how much of it relates to external conditioning. Assuming it's a biological imperative doesn't foster this kind of pre-parental reflection. Instead, the old mindset encourages us not to think too hard about pregnancy and parenthood, and just to do it like everyone else. The problem with people not giving this enough serious thought beforehand is that it confers parenthood on people who, in hindsight, realize that they should not have become parents and, given the choice again, would not choose to have children. Dr. Phil surveyed 20,000 parents, and one-third agreed with the statement, "If I knew what I know now, I probably wouldn't have started a family."[13]

Those parents may have come to this conclusion because their feelings shifted once they learned the realities of parenting. However, it can also mean that they didn't fully examine whether parenthood was right for them before going into it. And by "fully examine," I mean doing things like spending significant chunks of time with children of all ages and talking to parents about the less than positive aspects of parenthood. The latter can be tricky because pronatalist beliefs make it taboo for parents to admit any discontent. Living by the new Destiny Assumption will make it easier for parents to speak more openly about all aspects of parenthood, the good and the bad. This will be invaluable for those trying to decide whether parenthood is right for them.

In *I'm Okay, You're a Brat!: Setting the Priorities Straight and Freeing You From the Guilt and Mad Myths of Parenthood*, author Susan Jeffers, Ph.D. offers invaluable questions for mindful consideration. She says that parenthood can be the right choice if you can truly say "yes" to the following statements:

❖ *Even though my life is good now, I am ready to trade it in for a different one;*

❖ *I have experienced many of the things I have always wanted to experience, such as education, career goals, and travel;*

❖ *I realize having a child will mean putting certain aspects of my relationship and other areas of my life on the back burner until my child grows up; and*

❖ *I understand that the process of parenting can be difficult.*[14]

This kind of self-reflection needs to be undertaken when people feel the proverbial "urge" or "longing" to have children. When we realize we can't just chalk up that longing to instinct, we can better analyze the origins of our feelings. Here are other questions that need to be asked when people feel the "urge" or "longing": What is at the essence of this feeling of longing? Is my longing truly to raise a child, or is it another yearning I think the child will fill for me and my life?

It needs to become commonplace for men and women of child-bearing age to ask themselves these questions *before* children come on the scene. We have to better educate people so that rather than assume that parenthood will give them meaning in life, they know enough to figure out what purpose means to them. They can then identify how children fit into that picture. Such a process of self-exploration can help people realize that what they are truly longing for is not a child, but something else. The better we understand our motives and the more we recognize parenthood as a choice and not a biological imperative, the more likely we are to make the best choice for ourselves and our society.

Societal Acceptance

This Alternative Assumption also fosters social acceptance of a life that does not include parenthood. If we recognize that parenthood is a biological possibility, not biological destiny, what reason is there to judge people who opt not to have children? Fully adopting the Destiny Assumption also allows our society to let go of judgments of those who are child-"less"—those who do want children but are having trouble having them or can't have them. The supposition that giving birth is a biological imperative has put unnecessary pressure on want-to-be-parents to deliver on their reproductive destiny. Society has been all too good at reinforcing the old assumption with judgments like "you are somehow defective because you can't do what you are supposedly wired to do, so you are a 'failure.'" Focusing on pregnancy as something that *can* happen in life means we don't have to judge others when it doesn't happen. There is no reason to judge ourselves either. Dealing with the emotions that come with being childless is challenging enough. There is undoubtedly grief, but it's easier to work through and self-reflect on the best next course to take if society's judgments about not being able to get pregnant are not also an issue. This affords a healthier emotional environment in which to explore other options such as adoption or other ways to make children a meaningful part of one's life.

Whether we are parents, childfree, or childless, if we can stop drinking pronatal Kool-Aid, we can put parenthood and non-parenthood in their rightful social and cultural context. Either choice is equally legitimate and is equally acceptable and respectable. There's no reason to think otherwise.

3

THE NORMALITY
ASSUMPTION

Pronatalist assumptions speak not just to biology, but our psychology. We've been sold the message that parenthood is part of the natural progression toward healthy adulthood. In other words, parenthood is supposedly the normal path to becoming a mature adult man or woman. The pronatal assumption has been:

There is something wrong with you if you don't want children.

It's so common that even people who choose not to have children question whether there's something wrong with them. But consider how social norms—and the assumptions behind them—shift over time. In years past, women "grew up" when they married and left their parents' homes to live with their husbands. As women became more educated, people believed that going to college was really about getting a "Mrs." Degree—in other words, find a husband and have a family. This notion remains very similar today with just a tweak of a difference. Today, the supposed-to path for women sounds more like this: "Finish your degree, find a job, get married, and have a family." The "acceptable" timing may be changing, but the supposed-to flow to adulthood is the same. Men and women may marry later these days and start families later, but it's because the "finish the degree" and "find a job" or "obtain some level of financial stability" parts take longer. Many women today also choose to progress in their careers before having children. They may delay having children, but because many do eventually have them at some point, they are following the "normal" path. They and everyone else who eventually meet these milestones will follow the pronatalist protocol to adult normality. And components of this normality include psychological health, maturity, and a solid sense of identity.

A Sign of Psychological Health

Pronatalism has told us that having children is a sign of psychological health. However, the truth is that having children doesn't automatically mean we have our psychological selves together. If that were true, we'd see more troubled non-parents than parents in counseling rooms and prison cells. Pronatalism has promoted the myth that there's something psychologically wrong if you don't want kids. It has perpetuated the myth that the childfree come from troubled backgrounds and have emotional scars that lead them to say no to raising children. Research tells us that this isn't necessarily the case. Those who don't want children are no more likely to come from troubled backgrounds or have psychological wounds than those who grow up to become parents. Some childfree individuals do say negative experiences early in life factored into why they didn't want children, but not all. There's a host of other reasons why people choose not to have children.

Other reasons have to do with early life experiences that involve children and what they observed and learned from adult role models around them. Many childfree women talk about how babysitting made them realize they didn't like taking care of babies and children. Others talk about how they had a mentor, a role model, or even just an acquaintance who did not have children by choice, and how this exposed them to the idea that you didn't "have to have" children when you grew up. Many childfree men talk about watching their fathers (or in some cases their single mothers) struggle to provide for the family. They realized they never wanted to face that in their own adult lives, so they decided not to have children.

It often happens the other way—many people who had difficult childhoods grow up to *want* children. Lots of parents have a desire to raise kids in the way they wish they had been raised as a way to heal their own past, whether they are conscious of it or not. The healing comes from having the chance to parent the way they wish they had been parented, to do it "better" by giving their children what they wanted or deserved as children.

Many factors determine whether a person is a psychologically healthy adult. Having a child, in and of itself, does not confer psychological health. Not every parent has the self-esteem and strong sense of self that reflect psychological health in adulthood. And we all have our own road to attaining these things in our lives. The parenting process can be part of that road, but it doesn't have to be.

The Meaning of Maturity

The reality is that there are many paths to maturity. Adult maturity is also reflected in things like finding vocation, attaining financial independence, and showing financial responsibility. It means having emotional intelligence, understanding the value of humility over hubris, and finding meaning in life beyond materialism. It means seeing beyond ourselves to how our actions can impact others and our world.

People can have all of these things with or without children. The lives of mature adults who don't have children look very much like the lives of mature adults who are parents. The only difference is that they are not raising kids as part of their adult lives. Like many parents, they have jobs, careers, and mortgages. They have hobbies and social lives. They are devoted to friends and family. They contribute to their communities and the world through acts of service.

Just because people decide not to have children doesn't mean they aren't or won't become mature adults. The childfree know that the decision to bear children is one of the biggest decisions in life. They take it very seriously and carefully consider whether they want a child, whether they are emotionally and financially ready, and how it will affect their lives. This kind of consideration hardly exemplifies immaturity.

What does exemplify immaturity? People who jump into having a child without really thinking about what it will mean for them, their lives, or the child. People who have children without considering whether they are emotionally and financially ready are immature. People who have children even though they *know* they are not emotionally or financially ready are immature.

Now, the common belief is that once we are parents, we learn what it means to be "selfless." Our lives no longer revolve around us, and that is key to what it means to be a mature adult. So when we don't have kids by choice, we must not truly know what it means to be selfless. This is based on the erroneous assumption that adults who don't have children are living only for themselves. This just isn't the case.

Most people would agree that a life with purpose is one in which we endeavor to make some kind of meaningful contribution to the world. Pronatalism has advocated that "the" way to make that contribution is to have children. The reality is that there are many ways to do this without becoming a parent. Some childfree adults contribute directly to the lives of children in vocations that revolve around children, through volunteer work with children, or by playing a supportive role in the lives of children in their extended families. Those with no children give of themselves in a myriad of ways to children (as aunts, uncles, mentors)—to their families, communities, churches, and to larger social and political causes. Just because they aren't parents doesn't mean they think only of themselves. The myth that the childfree are selfish just serves to uphold pronatalism and keep parenthood on a pedestal.

How *parents* can be selfish is just not talked about enough. Being selfish can start with the decision to have the child. What's at the heart of the decision is the *parents' desire* to have and raise a child. It starts with what the parents want for themselves. It's selfish if would-be parents are not financially and emotionally ready, and they have a child anyway. Why do parents have the child anyway? So the child can fulfill some need of *theirs*. Pronatalism may have told us that parenthood is a selfless act, but as a report published by the Commission on Parenthood's Future and the Institute for American Values says, children can be "…commodities we commission to appease adult desires," instead of "vulnerable creatures with individual human dignity, whose needs must come first."[1]

Even some parents agree that having another child just because the parents didn't get the sex they wanted with the last one is more about them and what they want than anything else. It's also selfish when parents know what to do in terms of raising their children and don't, such as not giving them good nutrition, love and nurturing, praise, and discipline. In a nutshell, parents can be selfish whenever they think of themselves first, at the expense of their children.

Thinking of themselves first also plays out when parents try to live their "unlived lives" through their children. This is when parents create expectations or even force their children to do things *they* always wanted to do and didn't (or tried and failed) or force children to be what *they* always wanted to be. Sending the message to children that it's somehow up to them to live the unlived life of their mother or father is hardly a selfless act. Selfless parenting focuses on the child, not on what the parent wants to get from the parental experience.

The selfishness can continue throughout the child's life. Consider the parents who pressure their adult children to give them grandchildren. The would-be grandparents have their reasons for wanting grandchildren in their lives, but whose lives are they thinking of first? Theirs. So parents of any age can be selfish when they promote what they want over the desires of their children.

The number of children people choose to have can also be seen as selfish when you consider sustainability and population issues in the world. Environmental impact comes with the birth of every child. Specialists like Chris Packham say if you are considering the global impact of your parenthood decision, have one or none.[2] Others put the limit at not going beyond the replacement of self, or two children per couple (and not reproducing again if the couple splits up and have future relationships). This debate aside, it's selfish when we decide how many children we want based solely on our own desires without taking into consideration the effect on the planet and those already living on it.

So just because people are parents doesn't automatically mean they have hit a level of maturity where they don't engage in selfish acts. Having children doesn't determine whether a person is selfish or not. Being selfish is when we do what we want, *despite* how it will affect others. And people can do this whether they have kids or not.

"Normal" Sense of Identity

What is "normal" also relates to how we form our sense of identity, or how we develop our sense of our adult selves. For many years, we've tied identity to gender. Womanhood has been seen as synonymous with motherhood. For years, theories of female gender identity have said that if a woman shuns motherhood, it's a sign of "abnormal" development of her female identity.

However, in the early 1990s, the feminist movement began to see it differently. In *Reconceiving Women,* Mardy Ireland notes that the era of "3rd Wave Feminism" viewed "motherhood as only one facet of female identity, and not central to the development of a woman's sense of her adult self."[3] Years later, despite pronatalist doctrine to the contrary, this view of female identity has remained. As writer Naomi Rockler-Gladen puts it, "Third Wave feminists are encouraged to build their own identities from the available buffet, and to not worry if the items on their plate are not served together traditionally. Women can unapologetically celebrate a plate full of entrée choices like soccer mom, career woman, lover, wife, lesbian, activist, consumer, girly girl, tomboy, sweetheart, bitch, good girl, princess, or sex symbol."[4] In other words, motherhood is but one of the entrée choices women can include as part of building their unique identity.

Feminists aren't the only ones who are challenging theories that say maternity is the cornerstone of a woman's mature adult identity. Women of every ideology do so directly every time they make a conscious choice not to have children. Since the 1970s, more women have been choosing not to make motherhood part of their identity. Ireland claims that "these women are giving birth to additional forms of female identity."[5] More and more women are showing us that motherhood isn't required for a strong sense of identity.

For men, "normal" male identity has not solely revolved around becoming a father, but it has been an important element of a man's sense of self, along with occupation or line of work. Like with women who choose not to become mothers, men who choose not to become fathers have been viewed as abnormal. People who hold this view wonder how a man could not want to be a father when procreative virility sits right at the top of what it means to be a man. When men choose not to become fathers, they, too, challenge the notion that fatherhood has to be part of a man's adult identity. They demonstrate that fatherhood is not required for a strong sense of identity as a man.

If motherhood and fatherhood aren't required elements of adult identity, what does make up normal adult identities? For years, the elements that define our identities have started with gender and the ways in which boys and girls and men and women are innately different. Our identities have been defined by gender-based, hard-wired characteristics. For example, women traditionally have been seen as having more of a natural capacity for empathy and more interpersonal sensitivity than men. Men have been seen as more logical and analytical than women.

However, there are those who would challenge the idea that we should develop a self-concept stemming from what supposedly makes men and women different. In *Delusions of Gender: How Our Minds, Society, and Neurosexism Create Difference*, Cordelia Fine discusses how gender differences might not exist as much as we think. She questions contemporary science's view as to how men and women are different. When we "follow the trail of contemporary science we discover a surprising number of gaps, assumptions, inconsistencies, poor methodologies, and leaps of faith" when it comes to explaining gender differences.[6] She lays out many research studies that reveal how cultural and social context, more than innate biological differences, drive the development of gender differences. She posits how easily socialization and gender stereotyping can become self-fulfilling prophecies in how we see and understand ourselves. In other words, "it is the salience of gender and gender-related norms, rather than the gender per se, that lead to differences between men and women."[7]

And gender norms and stereotypes drive how we perceive our identity. Fine contends that seeing our self-concept and who we think we are "supposed" to be through the gender lens is not necessarily accurate, but we make it true as a result of deeply embedded social and cultural influences. The norms and stereotypes run so deep that we believe them to be unquestionably true. This not only limits our sense of identity but influences us to try and be who we're not. Fine is on to the fact that basing identity on gender limits our identity to only those aspects of ourselves that relate to gender norms and stereotypical roles. When we base our identity on gender-based elements, other parts of ourselves get pushed aside, preventing a fuller sense of identity. We can also try to be the way we think we are supposed to be, even though, in reality, it isn't who we really are. For example, women are traditionally supposed to be the "nurturers." But the truth is not all women are natural nurturers. They think they're supposed to be this way, so they end up trying to be something they are not in order to be a "normal" woman. Basing our identity on gender expectations can take us farther from, not closer to, knowing who we are.

What if we take gender and the stereotypes to which we're supposed to adhere out of the identity equation? What would it then mean to have a "normal" sense of identity? Third Wave feminism would say to women, "It's yours to create." However, this is true for men, too. It would mean we could develop our sense of identity based on characteristics, traits, and roles that we feel are true expressions of ourselves and who we want to be in the world.

If we develop our sense of identity in this way, we expand identity to the concept of personal identity. It can include the idea of finding our "calling"—what we find ourselves being called to do in our lives, or what we feel drawn to create and contribute to the world. Finding our own personal identity through calling doesn't have to begin when we're adults. It can start early in life with our natural way of being, our personalities, characteristics, our gifts. It also starts with our curiosities—our intense interests, fascinations, even obsessions, from when we were young to those we have today. Allowing ourselves to truly follow our interests and the directions they take us can lead us to finding our own personal identity. We can then free ourselves from the confines of the life pronatalism tells us we're supposed to have.

Mardy Ireland takes the idea of calling further. She feels we can form our sense of identity from the "inner call toward an individual life."[8] We can find a deep sense of personal identity from how we create and live an "authentic" life—one that is all our own. Our identity is not stuck in gender stereotypes and is not limited to our parental roles or solely our occupations. A "normal" sense of identity can be a unique combination of ways of being, personality, and roles that, together, form a more complete human identity.

The Alternative Assumption

It is just as normal to not want children as it is to want them.

It's time to challenge what pronatalism tells us is "normal." This Alternative Assumption sends the message that people's lack of desire to parent does not stem from something they lack. They've simply made a different life choice. They've recognized that they can be fully mature men and women without becoming parents. The beauty of this Alternative Assumption is that it opens the door to expanding our identity beyond motherhood and fatherhood. It also frees us from having to form our identities based on gender role stereotypes and allows us to have a deeper sense of ourselves based on all of who we know we are, not who society tells us we are supposed to be. We can more freely create our own "normal," which starts with ourselves as a "person" first and not with our sex or our role as a parent, which only some of us are. This new mindset gives people social permission to uniquely express their own human individuality.

4

THE MARRIAGE
ASSUMPTION

Pronatalism has been alive and well in the marriage business for generations. What's been the long-held assumption about marriage?

The purpose of marriage is to have children.

The connection between marriage and childbearing goes back a long time in history and has its roots in Christian religion, which bonded marriage and procreation as far back as 50 AD. Marriage's social and legal history supported this bond for hundreds of years.

History of the Marriage &
Procreation Bond

To look at the origins of the marriage and procreation bond, we can go back as far as the Roman Empire when its first emperor, Caesar Augustus, ruled. Years of civil war had left Rome in a state of near lawlessness, and birthrates were on the decline.[1] In 18 BC, Augustus instituted the Augustan Laws, which were the first to include laws that encouraged people to have children by penalizing childlessness and giving benefits to families who had three or more children.[2]

By 50 AD, the church got in on the act. Between 50 AD and 400 AD, the Fathers of the Christian Church wrote a new "sexual order" that centered on procreative marriage.[3] At that time, the Christians were fighting for dominance over the Gnostics, who did not believe marriage was about procreation. In fact, some Gnostics did not believe in marriage at all. In the end, however, the Church Fathers won religious power and defined the Christian procreative marriage.

Church Fathers came to bond procreation and marriage in a number of ways. Genesis 1:28 bears the infamous words, "be fruitful and multiply." Christians studied Jewish sages who declared, "One without children is considered as though dead" and "he who does not engage in procreation is as if he diminished the Divine image."[4] In 400 AD, another Church Father, St. Augustine, wrote *The Good of Marriage*, which laid out a marital morality that lasted 1500 years. In it, he argued that the purpose of marriage is the "perpetuation of man."[5] From the 13th to the 20th centuries, people saw marriage as "the indissoluble bond between a man and woman arising from the reciprocal exchange of authority over the other's bodies for the procreation and proper nurture of children."[6]

The marriage-procreation bond was so strong that it connected men's and women's relationships with God himself. The Church believed even the word "procreation" meant collaborating with the creativity of God—that in parenthood people entered into the heart of creation and, with God, became "co-authors" of the person they produced.[7] The emphasis on procreation from Caesar Augustus as a way to increase birth rates had come a long way; it had become associated with the ultimate way to connect with the "divine."

Social & Legal Reinforcement of the Bond

The Church was not the only social institution pressuring people to have children. In 18th century America, pronatalist social controls were in full force as more people were needed to populate and help settle vastly unsettled territories in our country. In the 18th century, the average woman between the ages of 20 and 40 had about eight children.[8] In the 19th century, children remained important to the economy. They were the cheapest labor on farms, mines, and factories, so the more, the better. In the 20th century, anti-child labor laws and compulsory schooling took children out of the labor force. They then became critical to the economy as consumers. The post-World War II baby boom spurred a surging consumer economy. The more kids, the more products sold, and the stronger the economy. During the Cold War, progressive reformers saw children as "agents of social renewal."[9] According to a 2008 report by the National Marriage Project, the Cold War "called upon the young to educate themselves in order to beat Communism, win the space race, and spread democracy."[10] Like in times past, the message was the more children, the better.

In 1873, a gentleman named Anthony Comstock came at the marriage and procreation bond from another angle. A devout Christian, he adamantly believed that birth control promoted "lust and prostitution."[11] He went after the contraceptive industry, which ultimately resulted in Congress passing the Comstock Act. The law defined contraceptives as obscene and illicit, and it became a federal offense to distribute them. After this law passed, more states followed suit. If you were caught breaking this law, it meant sizable fines and/or imprisonment. Some states made any use of contraceptives illegal. In 1879, Connecticut passed a law making birth control illegal, even for married couples. If birth control was found in the privacy of their homes, they could end up going to jail for a year.

Anti-birth control laws remained the law of the land for about another 40 years. Banning contraception and its distribution meant more unprotected sex, which meant the birth of more children. The policy of "no contraception" mirrored what the Christian church professed and supported the bond between marriage and procreation made by centuries of political and religious history.

The Breakdown of the Bond

According to Allan Carlson, Ph.D., President of The Howard Center and Distinguished Fellow in the Family Policy Studies at the Family Research Council, the bond of marriage and procreation has broken down over the course of the 20th century.[12] A strong factor: the legalization of contraception. In 1918, birth control advocate Margaret Sanger challenged the Comstock Act by claiming it violated federal and state constitutions. In *New York v. Sanger*, she claimed that opening her birth control clinic was not illegal because the Comstock Act was unconstitutional. She won; the legal ruling, commonly called the "Crane decision" because it was written by Justice of the Court Frederick Crane, stated that birth control could be used for therapeutic purposes.

Then in 1936, the *United States v. One Package* case opened the door for the medical community to distribute contraceptives. It ruled that laws prohibiting Americans from importing contraceptive devices or items causing "unlawful abortion" did not apply to physicians who used the items to protect the health of patients.[13] But in 1965, *Griswold v. Connecticut* opened the door even wider. Estelle Griswold, Executive Director of the Planned Parenthood League of Connecticut at the time, and Dr. C. Lee Buxton, a physician and professor at the Yale School of Medicine, decided to test the constitutionality of the Connecticut law banning contraception. They opened a birth control clinic. They were tried and found guilty, and the conviction was upheld in the Appellate Division of the Circuit Court and by the Connecticut Supreme Court. Griswold appealed her conviction to the U.S. Supreme Court, which concluded that the 1879 Connecticut Statute was unconstitutional on the grounds that it violated the "right to marital privacy." Essentially, as Evan Wolfson states in *Why Marriage Matters*, this decision meant that "marriage is not just about procreation—indeed it is not necessarily about procreation at all."[14]

However, the right to privacy in *Griswold v. Connecticut* only applied to married relationships; in other words, only married couples could possess contraception. Seven years later, in 1972, *Eisenstadt v. Baird* finally extended the same contraceptive rights to unmarried people. Justice William Brennan held that, "If the right of privacy means anything, it is the right of the individual, married or single, to be free from unwarranted governmental intrusion into matters so fundamentally affecting a person as the decision whether to bear or beget a child."[15]

These rulings took the eye off procreation and on to individual rights regarding intercourse and reproduction. In the context of marriage, they made it legally legitimate for marriage not to be inextricably connected to children. As Allan Carlson writes, "Can we still defend the purpose of marriage as procreation? No, not in the current Constitutional climate."[16]

The social context of the timing of *Griswold v. Connecticut* supported the legal unraveling of the bond between marriage and procreation. Although the FDA had approved birth control pills for contraceptive use in 1960, married women began to use them in droves as a family planning tool after *Griswold v. Connecticut*. In the 1970s, laws finally allowed single women to legally use a highly effective method of contraception and have more control over their reproductive lives.

It was also the time of the rise of feminism and women's rights. In 1963, Betty Friedan's groundbreaking book, *The Feminine Mystique*, spurred society to question for the first time the long-held notion that women found their identity and fulfillment in life by becoming wives and mothers. These times opened the doors for women to explore self-realization beyond motherhood and go beyond the thinking that marriage and bearing children represented the core purpose of women's existence. With birth control more popular than ever before and more women delaying childbearing as they worked outside the home, women continued to see that there was more to marriage than motherhood. The expansion of women's identities made women begin to realize that the reason they wanted to get married went beyond having children. They could marry to build a life with their partner that included parenthood, but that wasn't at the core of their union. Men and women were marrying first and foremost for love. Now, marrying for love was not a new idea at this time. It had been over 200 years in the making beginning in the 18th century.[17] However, the age of women's empowerment inspired the real evolution of this view of the purpose of marriage.

While the purpose of marriage has expanded socially, many modern day theologians still hold the view that the purpose of marriage is to have children. Not all maintain this view, however. Some theologians have a more balanced view of marriage, which has supported the weakening of the marriage and procreation bond. For example, even though the first chapter of Genesis says to "be fruitful and multiply," not all theologians agree that it means every Christian marriage is obligated to have children. According to Kenneth Magnuson, University of Cambridge Ph.D. and professor of Christian Ethics, the language in the first chapter of Genesis can be interpreted in terms of children being more of a "blessing" from God, not a "mandate" that couples must meet for God.[18] The Book of Genesis doesn't speak to procreation anywhere else, and in Genesis 2, it celebrates the man and woman's "one-flesh" relationship, which some theologians interpret as speaking to the union or companionship purpose of marriage.

As far back as 300-400 AD, many theologians were suspicious of and looked upon sexual desire with distain, pushing procreation as the primary purpose of marriage as a way to justify sexual intercourse. Others thought differently. Theologian Lactantius didn't preach procreation as the only thing that justified marriage, and he believed that sexual desire and pleasure were gifts from God. Different Christian religions grew to agree. Twentieth century theologians such as Deitrich Bonhoeffer and Karl Barth advanced Lactantius' thinking, saying that sexual desire is good because it fosters "procreation, union and companionship in marriage."[19] They professed that part of marriage is not founded upon the purpose of reproduction but on the union of man and woman."[20] Barth thought that putting too much emphasis on procreation took away from marriage's purpose as a union between man and woman. He believed that "procreation should not be allowed to take priority over marital companionship and bodily union." Bonhoeffer went on to say that when "procreation is impossible, marriage is not in any way deficient."[21]

The Alternative Assumption

People marry as a way to bring them happiness and fulfillment in life.

These legal, social, and even religious developments show us we are well on our way to fully letting go of the old pronatalist assumption regarding the purpose of marriage. Recent research supports this reality; it tells us that people no longer believe the institution of marriage most importantly revolves around having children. Not even close.

According to a 2007 report by the Pew Research Center (PRC), "there has been a distinct weakening of the link between marriage and parenthood."[22] In 1990, PRC surveyed people about what is very important to a marriage, including areas such as faithfulness, happy sexual relationship, sharing household chores, adequate income, good housing, shared religious beliefs, shared tastes and interests, children, and agreement on politics. At that time, respondents ranked having children third in importance. In 2007, PRC gave the public the same list, and this time, children ranked next to last. The 2007 survey found that, "by a margin of nearly three-to-one, Americans say that the main purpose of marriage is the 'mutual happiness and fulfillment' of adults rather than the 'bearing and raising of children.'" This research indicates that we've moved on from times past and that we see marriage as more about the relationship between the partners than the children they may or may not have together.

So why is it still so common to ask newly married couples when they plan to start a family? And continue to ask this question as they go along in their marriage? Why, more often than not, do couples get pressure from family and friends to have children? In other words, why are children so expected if having children is not the driving force behind why people marry? Because pronatalism remains a cultural and social force. A pronatalist would look at the Pew research and say that if the purpose of marriage is to experience mutual happiness and fulfillment, part of experiencing that happiness and fulfillment together should eventually include parenthood.

In today's pronatalist world, do most people agree that having children makes for a happy and fulfilling marriage? Recent figures suggest that some people do, but the numbers are falling. In 1990, PRC reported that 65 percent of adults said children are important to a successful marriage. In 2007, that number dropped to 41 percent.[23] The growing number of people in childfree marriages would agree with the majority who don't think children are important to a successful marriage. They know that parenthood is not necessary to have a happy and fulfilled marriage.

In fact, more than likely, those in childfree marriages feel that parenthood would *not* be the best thing for their marriage. One of the biggest concerns many couples have today when trying to decide whether to have children is how it will affect their marriage. They ask themselves, "With things going so well right now, why risk jeopardizing it?" More and more couples end up deciding that their relationship is more important to them than introducing the experience of parenthood to that relationship.

When a couple decides to remain a family of two, what makes their marriage happy, fulfilling, and successful? From the interview research for my book, *Families of Two,* three components stand out most. First, the couple shares mutual interests. In the sharing of those interests, childfree couples create things together that fulfill them individually and together, and those things often make a positive impact on others and their communities. The childfree engage in an endless array of acts of creation. The one act of creation they don't engage in is the conception of children.

Despite the perpetual myth that the childfree don't like children, many happy and fulfilled childfree married couples are devoted aunts and uncles, and they play special roles in the lives of their friends' children. The marriage does allow room for time with children, just not their own. The couples have decided the role they want children to play in their lives together, and their families, friends, and children reap the benefit of their involvement.

Happy couples who don't become parents by choice show us why it's time to take parenthood out of what it means to experience a fulfilling marriage. They show by example how a rich marriage is not defined by whether children are part of it or not. It's defined by each couple, and how they determine what a successful marriage means to them. Every couple needs to figure this out, and when they do, it creates a relationship that's all their own. Just like there aren't two other people in the world like each of them, there is no other relationship like theirs. They are the ones who hold the unique keys to their marriage going the distance.

More and more people, parents and not, are letting go of pronatalist notions when it comes to marriage. They realize that children aren't automatic components of a marriage, or a happy one at that. To truly let go means letting go of all of the expectations we have been taught to have around marriage and parenthood. If we don't expect all couples to have children, there's no reason to ask them when they're going to "start trying." Nor will there be any reason to pressure couples to have children.

Without expectations, the bond between marriage and parenthood is fully released from pronatalist grips. Couples are free to choose whether they want parenthood to be part of their marital experience. Without expectations, we can also let go of the other pronatalist belief that parenthood should be part of every person's experience of life.

5

THE RIGHT TO REPRODUCE ASSUMPTION

One of pronatalism's strongest assumptions has had to do with a person's individual right to reproduce. The assumption has long been:

Everyone has the right to have children.

Today, the notion that everyone has the right to have a child does not just relate to those who are biologically capable of having children. Thanks to advances in medical technology, it has extended to those who have trouble conceiving biologically. For example, these days many people believe their health insurance should cover the services they need to conceive, such as in vitro fertilization. And a good number of states do just that; they have laws requiring insurance coverage for infertility treatment. The idea that everyone has a "right" to bear a child and that nothing should stand in the way of that has remained doggedly fixed for a number of reasons.

Why It's So Ingrained

For centuries, pronatalism has driven the "strong societal consensus in favor of the right to procreate."[1] It promotes the notions that it's only natural for humans to want to produce offspring, and it's every person's natural born right to produce those offspring. Even more strongly, pronatalist thinking says that it's our duty to our lineage and the world to have children; it's not only something we are all here to do, but also our obligation to perpetuate our family line and the human species.

This assumption goes beyond pronatalism's set of beliefs to ideas in the founding documents of our country. The Declaration of Independence sets forth the idea that we all have the right to "life, liberty and the pursuit of happiness." Part of having the freedom to live the life we choose can certainly be interpreted as the right to have children. The Fifth Amendment of the Constitution reinforces this idea with law. It offers protections to our "life, liberty, or property" and maintains that we can't be deprived of any of these things without due process of law.[2] The courts have recognized that "liberty" under the due process clause in the Constitution includes the right "to marry, establish a home, and bring up children."[3] In other words, the government or anyone else can't interfere with or prevent people from having children. This individualistic right doesn't exist, however, without great costs to society.

The Costs of It Being Everyone's Right

Society pays hefty social, psychological, and financial costs as a result of the belief that anyone should be able to have children. Because society condones having children whenever people want to, many people have children before they are emotionally or financially ready. Take teens, for example. Each year, almost 750,000 U.S. women between the ages of 15 and 19 become pregnant. In 2006, 59 percent of these pregnancies ended in birth; in other words, almost 60 percent of pregnant teens this age become mothers. And overall, 10 percent of all births in the United States are to girls 19 years old or younger.[4]

But it isn't just teenagers who aren't prepared to parent. Many adults have children before they are ready as well. In both cases, this all too often leads to unfit parenting. We see evidence of unfit parents every day in the news. Parental abuse statistics are unnerving. According to HealthTeacher, a health curriculum organization designed for teachers and health educators, "every 13 seconds, a child is abused or neglected. One in four girls and one in seven boys when they are children will experience some form of sexual abuse." And "77 percent of child abuse perpetrators are parents."[5] The psychological and emotional costs to the children in these situations are staggering, and all too often, affect their lives for years to come.

Unfit parent abuse and neglect also takes the form of outright physical abandonment. Surprisingly, laws in all 50 states allow parents to do this without punishment. All states have adopted a form of the "Safe Haven Infant Protection Act." Within 30 days after birth, parents(s) can drop their baby off at any police station or hospital, and never come back. The law even has a slogan: "No shame. No blame. No names." If a parent doesn't come back in 21 days, the State terminates the right of the parents and allows for adoption. This could be construed as good news because the child will hopefully end up with a home. However, when the birth parents' rights end, they're absolved from any child support responsibility for their child.[6]

Abuse, neglect, and abandonment by unfit parents land many kids in foster care. In 2009, almost 424,000 children were in foster care, mostly due to abuse and neglect.[7] Worse than this, more unfit parents than one might think make their children go away for good. According to the American Anthropological Association, "three to five children a day are killed by their parents. Homicide is one of the leading causes of death of children under age four."[8] The Save the Babies Foundation indicates that "nearly five infants under the age of one are killed in the U.S. each week."[9]

Not only do the harmed children who survive go through life suffering heavy emotional and psychological costs, but many of them grow up to harm society. According to HealthTeacher, "abuse during childhood increases the likelihood of arrest as a juvenile by 53 percent, arrest as an adult by 38 percent and the likelihood of violent crime by 38 percent." Additionally, "being abused or neglected in childhood increases the likelihood of arrest for females by 77 percent."[10]

Who pays for the costs of unfit parents and their harmed children? We do. Starting with teen pregnancy, according to an analysis by The National Campaign to Prevent Teen and Unplanned Pregnancy, national costs (federal, state, and local) of teen childbearing were "at least *$10.9 billion*" in 2008. The cost of public funding includes expenses like health care, foster care, and lost tax revenues.[11] Child abuse costs are far higher. In 2007, Prevent Child Abuse America conservatively estimated the annual costs of child abuse and neglect at *$103.8 billion*. The estimate is conservative because it only includes costs associated with the victims and doesn't include costs of intervention or treatment services for those doing the harm. It also doesn't take into account costs associated with the large number of child victims who require medical examinations or outpatient treatment for injuries not serious enough to require hospitalization.[12] It doesn't factor in future behaviors either. Abused children have higher odds of engaging in substance abuse, which turns into treatment service costs. They also have a higher probability of engaging in unprotected sexual activities, which takes us right back to the high public costs of teen pregnancy.

Abuse and neglect are the most common reasons children end up in foster homes. The economic impact analysis by Prevent Child Abuse America indicates there are "over $33 billion in direct costs for foster care services, hospitalization, mental health treatment, and law enforcement. Indirect costs of over $70 billion include loss of productivity, as well as expenditures related to chronic health problems, special education, and the criminal justice system."[13]

Taxpayers pick up the tab associated with children abandoned in accordance with Safe Haven Laws. There are hospital costs, which can get very expensive depending on the health issues of the child. There are also foster care costs, so it's part of the larger $33 billion dollar foster care cost pie. Then, there are the public costs associated with parents who opt out of their financial responsibilities to their children. The federal government has a Child Support and Enforcement Program that distributes funds to the states, which are used to "locate non-custodial parents, establish paternity when necessary, and establish and enforce orders for support." In 2009, the federal government spent *$4.3 billion* attempting to ensure that people paid their child support.[14] And tragically, there are federal, state, and local court costs associated with cases involving parental child abuse and homicide.

Clearly, we pay a heavy price for subscribing to the idea that it's everyone's right to have children, regardless of whether people are emotionally, financially, or psychologically ready to have them. And clearly, too many children, the parents themselves, and society are harmed as a result of this unquestioned right.

The Alternative Assumption

Parenthood is a privileged right.

In our society, driving is a privilege. Before we can get our driver's license, we all have to show we can drive competently and safely. Why? If we aren't able to drive well, it will result in harm to others. Because parenthood can potentially cause great harm to children and society, and because it's arguably the most important job in the world, why don't we have the same attitude when it comes to having children? Parenthood needs to be seen as a privileged right, not an automatic right.

The Myth that Parenthood Comes Naturally

Even with all of the harm that comes from treating parenthood as an unquestioned right, there's still the strong belief that parenthood is supposed to come naturally to everyone and that there's a strong connection between the ability to give birth and the ability to parent. As Keli Goff, author and contributing editor at the TheLoop21.com has pointed out, "Parenting, the most important job in the world, is treated as something you don't need any knowledge or preparation to do well." And the "mere suggestion that people can actually improve their capabilities as a parent through education and effort (and should want to) continues to be perceived as taboo."[15] Why? Because it is just supposed to come naturally. This just isn't the case.

Agreeing with Ellen Peck, *The Parent Test: How to Measure and Develop Your Talent for Parenthood* co-author William Granzig also believed that there are important differences between procreation and parenthood—that "Gestation is biological. Birth is biological. But parenthood is psychological in its application."[16] So why do we continue to think that it's supposed to come naturally? Pronatalism. If it comes naturally, it isn't going to be that difficult. And if we believe that's the case, what are we more likely to do? Just what pronatalism touts: Have children.

When you take the pronatalist veil away, the truth is that the process of parenting does not come naturally. Like any job, it requires certain skills and aptitudes. Having it begin to feel "natural" comes as a result of acquiring the skills necessary for successful parenting. It's also true that for many parents, it never feels natural or never gets easy, even with a great deal of effort. We need to see parenthood for what it really is—something that not everyone is cut out for, that isn't right for everyone. How do we best determine this? It starts with education.

Mandated Teen Education

To begin treating reproduction as a privileged right, young people need serious education about parenthood early in life. Parenthood education does already exist in some schools, but it's often not mandatory. In Texas, however, it is required. In 2007, Texas passed a law that requires parenting and paternity awareness (p.a.p.a) curriculum to be taught in high schools. The p.a.p.a curriculum deals with the "rights, responsibilities, and realities of parenting." It addresses the benefits of having both parents involved in a child's life and covers relationship skills, the legal realities of child support, the financial and emotional challenges of single parenting, and relationship violence prevention.[17]

Other schools offer life skills classes with unit(s) on parenting. A more popular "parenting 101" unit is called the Egg Baby Project, where students (younger than high school) pretend they are parents by taking care of a boiled egg for several days. They have to take it everywhere with them, even to the restroom. If they can't take the egg baby with them, they have to get the egg a babysitter. If they crack their egg, they lose points. If the egg gets completely cracked, students are even required to give a eulogy in front of their class. Reports say that it's a constructive way for students to "realize the responsibilities that come along with being a parent" and that it's a very big job.[18]

More commonly, though, life skills classes, particularly at the high school level, don't include parenthood awareness modules. They are more often designed to address the substance abuse and violence prevention issues of young adults. Studies indicate that if parenthood education is offered, it will pave the way for better quality parenting down the line. One such study, done by U.K. researchers Richard Layard and Judith Dunn, included 35,000 people. It is considered "the most far-reaching inquiry into childhood in the U.K." The resulting report, "A Good Childhood: Searching for Values in a Competitive Age," advocates education on parenting, relationships, and child development as a way to improve the quality of parenting. It stresses that good parenting education should occur before a "baby is conceived" and that before the child is born, "the parents should be fully informed of what is involved in bringing up a child."[19]

This kind of education can help make better parents, not just in the U.K. but anywhere. However, it needs to go further than the realities and skills of parenting. In fact, teaching the parenting how-to's puts the cart before the horse. Instead, it should start with young people exploring their *interest* in parenting. Curriculum needs to help them think about these kinds of questions: Do I think I want to be a parent one day? Why? Given what I know about myself, my personality, and what I like and don't like, do I think I would be good at it?

In other words, before the skill orientation, young people need to explore their motives and desire for having children and their aptitude to parent one day. Part of shifting to the idea that parenthood is a privileged right includes making it a given that we all look hard at whether it's right for us. And it isn't too early for those of childbearing age—or almost—to be exposed to this idea. Since they are not too young to face unintended pregnancy at this age, they are certainly not too young to begin self-examination about this important life decision. Why doesn't parenthood education cover this kind of thing? Because pronatalism teaches us that we are all supposed to eventually become parents. It's assumed that parenthood is just part of life when you grow up. Instead, we need to introduce the idea early that parenthood is not something everyone does, and not everyone wants to have parenthood be part of their adult life.

It's also assumed that you will have your own biological children. Adoption is seen as less attractive. Young people need to be given an entirely different orientation to this topic—one that begins with learning about the impact that having children has on the world. They need to learn how bearing offspring affects the population of their own country and that of the world and how population growth affects natural resources. They should also be taught that adoption should not be the last resort and that it's a way to have the parenthood experience, while contributing to the life of a child who needs a home while not adding to the world's population issues.

Kids also need to be taught about the reality that not everyone is cut out to be parents, adoptive or not, and that if you're not, that's just fine. They need to know that it's okay for them to one day decide they don't want to become parents. In high school, it's probably too early for students to know for sure whether they will one day want children, but it isn't too early for them to reflect on what they want to do with their lives once they are adults and what they envision for their future. They aren't too young to explore their level of desire to eventually become a parent or not and to understand that parenthood is not everyone's prerequisite for a happy life. They can begin to ask themselves what happiness in life means to them and explore how parenthood might fit into this picture. Widening the range of the curriculum to include this kind of reflection, along with providing an honest look at the challenges, downsides, and skills needed to successfully parent will not only make for more effective parenting education, but also model for students the value of educating themselves about one of the most important decisions they will ever make.

This kind of comprehensive education program should be mandated for all schools, public and private. It should be set up so that if students don't complete it, they don't graduate. In an era of economic challenge, people will likely balk at the public costs for this kind of program. However, if we put these costs against the billions of dollars we already incur from the impacts of teen parents and unfit adult parents, plus the harm done to children and others in society, it's easy to see that this is a wise investment. If we help make kids smarter earlier about the choices they make when it comes to parenthood, they will make better choices. *If* they choose to become parents, they will be less likely to become unfit parents and contributors to the costs to our society as a result.

Adult Parent Education

Once young people become adults, if they decide they want children, there are plenty of resources to help them prepare for this experience. There are hundreds of books for parents to be, online parenting discussion forums, and, in some communities, parents-to-be classes. Once the children are born, there are also many places for parents to turn for help, from books to classes to online courses to "parent coaching" services. An offshoot of the executive coaching industry, the "parent coaching" industry has been growing in the last several years, particularly for parents who can afford to pay the pricey hourly rates for this service.[20] There are also many online resources for parents looking to adopt or become foster parents.

There are educational programs that are mandated but tend to only have the goal of remedying bad parenting. For example, in early 2010, the Parent Accountability Act went into effect in California. Judges have the option of ordering parents to go to training when their kids are convicted of gang crimes for the first time. Similar legislative efforts have occurred in other states, such as Florida and Indiana. Other court-mandated classes, such as the Parent Project, help counsel parents on dealing with their kids skipping school, taking drugs, or getting involved in gang life.[21]

Make no mistake: These kinds of programs serve the public good. But there's a fundamental problem with this approach. It's help *after the fact*. Parents are seeking help either when the baby is already on the way or after the child is already here, when the problems already exist. It would be far better to invest these resources in pre-pregnancy parenting education programs to help people think through why they want to become parents and whether they have the skill sets parenting requires.

The Aptitude for Parenthood

In the late 70s, Ellen Peck and William Granzig, authors of *The Parent Test*, came up with a way to think about parenthood that we'd be wise to adopt today. Consider how the concept of aptitude can be used to help predict whether people have the qualities to be good in a particular occupational field. Peck and Granzig suggest we apply that concept to parenting. They argue that that "the concept of aptitude can help those interested in becoming parents predict their probable success and happiness in that role."[22] Just like there are people who are not cut out for certain kinds of jobs and occupations, from an aptitude point of view, "it is reasonable to assume that there are people who are not cut out to be parents."[23]

In other words, some people have a greater aptitude for parenthood than others. In the realm of parent education, we are sorely lacking in ways to assess people's aptitude for parenthood before they take on this job. We are also sorely lacking in ways to educate adults about various ways to use this aptitude other than to have their own children. But we do this routinely with career aptitudes. Take the example of musical aptitude. People with high musical aptitude don't all end up doing the same thing with that aptitude. Some people find they enjoy research, others play in a band, and still others decide they are best suited to become music critics. With parenthood, we don't do this; people don't assess their aptitude for this job before they have kids, and they are not required to figure out what ways would be best for them to use this aptitude if they do have it. As Peck and Granzig argue, aptitude for parenthood can vary greatly. People don't have the chance to realize that they "may have an aptitude for dealing sensitively and patiently with one child but not with more." We don't find out if we "may be able to handle parenthood in an urban setting with convenient day care but not in a small town as a 24 hour a day parent." We don't have a way to find out whether we "may be impatient with infants but superb at stimulating the thinking of a preschooler." We don't have a way to find out whether we are best using our parent aptitude in some way other than becoming a parent, such as teaching or vocational counseling. And we don't have a structured way to seriously assess whether it's too early to use our aptitude for parenthood just yet because of too many unfulfilled dreams and commitments.[24]

Peck and Granzig break down aptitude into six "components of capability" as it relates to parenting. They look at this from a couple's point of view:

1. Expectations: What expectations do we have about parenthood? How realistic are they?

2. Resources: How do our resources measure up to the generally

accepted requirements for the job of parenthood?

3. Skills: Do we have the needed skills for the job of parenthood? If not, how can they be developed?

4. Motivations: How strongly and for what reasons do we want to enter the process of parenting?

5. Traits: How well do we match the personal characteristics of happy, successful parents?

6. Interests: How sincere are our interests in all the elements of parenthood?[25]

Today, rarely if ever, do would-be parents think seriously about these questions, crucial as they are. It's because they don't know to do so. And that's because of the assumption that parenting is a right rather than a privilege for those who can do it well. In today's society, it's imperative that it become the norm for would-be parents to be required to show they can meet these kinds of components of capability before they take on the incredibly important job of parenthood.

Mandated Parent Qualification Certification

Everyone needs to pass a driver's test and get a license to drive legally. Certain professions also require licensure or certifications to practice. It's time to do the same with parenthood. Whether they want to bear their own children or adopt, would-be parents should be required to complete a mandated, federal or state-funded parent qualification program before they have the right to raise children. For this discussion, let's call it a "Parent Qualification Certification" program or PQC. It should be set up so that completion needs to occur at least one year before a person becomes a parent. In other words, completion needs to happen *before* the onset of pregnancy.

The program would be developed by experts from a range of

relevant fields such as education, counseling, family relations, child psychology, obstetrics, gynecology, reproductive health, and public health. This was the case with the experts who conceptualized and developed *The Parent Test* described in Peck and Granzig's book. They created a series of questionnaires that tell people how they "compare (in terms of resources, traits, skills, interests, and expectations) with parents who have felt happy and successful in their role" as parents.[26] Other kinds of aptitude tests do the same. The "successful practitioners of the profession of parenthood" saw themselves as good parents and were identified by others as good parents. They also had entered into what are "generally considered to be parenthood's most difficult years: all had at least one child who had reached mid-adolescence."[27] Their answers to the questionnaires were compared to admittedly unhappy parents, many of whom unequivocally stated that given the choice again, they would not have children. The development of the questionnaires was based on the differences in responses between the two groups.

The experts developed a multitude of items that delved into these areas:

Do I have the basics—health, maturity, home, money?

Am I interested in children? Do I find the tasks involved in child raising at different ages interesting?

Why am I applying for this job? To what extent are my reasons egotistical (e.g., to have my child do what I wanted to do but didn't), compensatory (e.g., to make up for lack of satisfaction or fulfillment in other areas of life), conforming (e.g., to please my parents) and emotional (e.g., to have the satisfaction of giving myself to someone else)?

Am I as clear as I can be about my "discrepancies of expectations"—the difference between what I think is going to happen when I become a parent and what is really going to happen, e.g., changes in social patterns, closeness with spouse, sexuality, impact on career, old age support?

Do I have the skills a parent needs, e.g., ability to nurture, teach, discipline, deal with disputes, be organized, and manage (to name just a few)?

Do I have the traits a parent needs, e.g., patience, independence, practicality, generosity (also just to name a few that were identified)?

The questionnaires were designed to be scored and discussed. A mandated PQC program can be set up similarly. It can be developed by experts who design it based on differences between happy and good parents and unhappy parents. Those who think they want to be parents will go through a program that involves self-assessment, plus a discussion of this assessment and how their parenthood aptitude scores need to improve before they become parents.

The program would also include a segment on understanding one's personal psychology—to be able to answer yes to: "Am I sufficiently aware of my core psychological and emotional issues?" Before we become parents, we need to become aware of our childhood wounds and psychological weaknesses. As humans, we carry emotional hurts. We need to have some level of self-understanding of these hurts and related emotional issues before we begin raising children. If we don't have this self-awareness, our parenting and our children will suffer. We see the more serious effects of this lack of awareness every day when we read the many stories about physical and emotional parental abuse, child abandonment, and harm.

Like at the student level, a PQC program also needs to include education on the "planetary harm" that comes from bringing more biological children into the world. As the alternative Offspring Assumption discusses, would-be parents need to become very aware of how having biological children affects population growth, not only for their own country but for population growth as a whole. Beyond that, they need to be taught how population growth affects the environment and how parenting the children who are already here can be a powerful way to parent while simultaneously contributing to population stabilization efforts.

A PQC program is so important that it needs to be set up with strong incentives for people to complete it. For example, it could be set up so that if the mother and father of a child did not complete the PQC program at least a year before the birth of that child, they would not receive tax credits for the child or any child that follows. It could also be set up so that non-certified parents would not be eligible for just any kind of health care insurance plan; they would be eligible but have limited family program options. There would be exceptions, such as for pregnancies that occurred as a result of rape. And like any certification that needs to be "renewed," the PQC program could require parental completion of a supplemental self-assessment and ability development program, such as before the births of subsequent children.

No doubt, some might initially balk at the costs associated with a mandated PQC program, just as they might balk at the cost of expanded parenthood education at the high school level. However, concerns about the costs of developing and running such a program need to be put against the billions in costs we pay in the current environment, where anyone can have a child based on biological capability (or fertility treatment success) alone. We all see the many ways our society pays the price for this. The costs to administer a PQC Department, for example, would be less than the *billions* of dollars in costs we are already incurring as a result of dealing with the effects of unfit parents. As a result of a PQC, the number of unfit parents would also decrease, thus decreasing the billions we pay in bad parenting costs.

We can all agree that parenthood is an important job, arguably the most important job of all. We screen people for jobs, sometimes intensely given the nature of the job, its impact, and potential capacity to harm others. The job of parenting deserves the same kind of screening for the good of the parents, the potential children, and society. The experts are out there to develop a program to do this. Parenthood deserves to be treated not as an automatic right, but as a privileged right. This kind of program would be a very concrete way to acquire that right.

Punitive Measures for Unfit Parenting

Even with a mandated Parent Qualification Certification program, there will be those who don't complete it or who don't exhibit sufficient parenthood aptitude and have biological or adoptive children anyway. Those who show severe levels of unfitness, such as recurring child alimony non-payment; physical, emotional, or sexual abuse; parental substance abuse; neglect; abandonment or homicide, should temporarily lose their right to reproduce. Even in a democratic society like ours, rights are taken away when people harm others. We do this in our legal and prison system. The same should happen for unfit parents. There must be ways to prevent unfit parents from continuing to harm children and society, financially and socially.

One punitive measure that could be taken with extremely unfit parents would be to require long term birth control. A way to do this for severely unfit fathers may well be on the horizon. There is a new method of birth control for men called RISUG ("reversible inhibition of sperm under guidance"). RISUG consists of two tiny injections into the scrotum that result in 100 percent birth control protection for ten years or more. The injections take about 15 minutes and have no side effects. The RISUG technique injects a positively charged nontoxic polymer into a section of the vas deferens (the tiny tubes that carry sperm to the penis, where they then mix with prostate fluids to form semen), which chemically "incapacitates the sperm," making them incapable of fertilizing an egg. Sperm have a negative charge, and when they pass the positively charged polymer, the charge differential from the polymer "zaps" them 100 percent of the time.[28]

Here is how it could work for severely unfit fathers. RISUG is completely reversible. Severely unfit fathers could be required to take the injections, and when they prove they are no longer in the severely unfit category (as set forth in the PQC program), they could be given another injection that reverses the positive polymer effect, after which they would again be able to reproduce. The predictions are that RISUG will be available in as little as two years.

There are two highly effective long term contraceptive options that would work for women in this situation. One is an intrauterine device (IUD). There are two types of IUDs—one is a copper-containing IUD that works by preventing sperm from reaching the Fallopian tubes. It is over 99 percent effective, and lasts for at least 10 years. There is also a levonorgestrel-releasing IUD which works by thickening the cervical mucus and thinning the endometrium (the lining of the uterus). It can be left in place for up to five years and has the same high effectiveness rate as the copper-containing IUD. Severely unfit mothers, just like unfit fathers, could be required to use this method of long term birth control until they are deemed out of the severely unfit category.[29]

This may sound radical to people who have grown up immersed in a pronatalist culture that allows anyone who is biologically capable to become a parent. But it isn't radical in a society that treats parenthood as a privileged right. In this kind of society, those convicted of serious offenses, such as child abuse, abandonment, or homicide charges involving children would be refused the reversibility option. Either they should be required to remain on long term birth control or be sterilized. If they have been charged with crimes against children, their privilege to parent should be taken away for good. Part of treating parenthood as a privileged right means those who have been convicted of crimes against children should not have a child or a subsequent child.

Like teen education, a mandated PQC program that includes long term birth control oversight to prevent badly unfit parents from having more children would require federal/state funding for implementation. Again, the costs to society of unfit parents are so much greater. It's time we start spending money to prevent harm to children and society rather than billions on cleaning up the messes we've failed to prevent.

Positive Effects of Certifying Parenthood

A decrease in teen pregnancies

Mandated programs at the high school level would help young people become better educated about themselves and parenthood (and its prevention, e.g., contraception education), which would help them make better choices for themselves earlier in life. If it were set up so that teens would not be eligible for a PQC program until they had graduated high school, this would also encourage them not to become pregnant until they could age-qualify, which could positively contribute to a decrease in teen pregnancy.

A decrease in unintended pregnancies

Because there would be serious incentives to become a certified parent way before getting pregnant, people would be motivated to prevent unplanned pregnancy. They would not want to potentially sacrifice tax benefits and health care options.

Fewer unfit parents

With this kind of education, parents would know going in why they wanted children, that they were having them for the right reasons, and that they had high enough skills to effectively raise their children. Knowing these things would better set them up to enjoy and do well at raising children.

Promotion of "parenthood-optional" values

The concept of "parenthood is a choice in life" would be taught early, as would the demystification of the pronatalist idea that it's something everyone should do. Those who don't have a high enough aptitude and don't want children enough to raise that aptitude wouldn't feel something is "wrong" with them for not choosing to become parents. Nor would those who *have* the aptitude but don't have the desire to have children. The cultural context around parenthood would allow for everyone to choose what is best for them and not be judged for that choice.

Decreased social and financial harm to society

Treating parenthood as a privilege would shift the cost responsibility from dealing with the aftermath of unfit parents to preventing them in the first place. The costs to take preventative measures to ensure effective parenting as much as possible would result in far fewer costs from the harm done by unfit parents.

Reduction of harm to the well-being of many children

This may be the most important result of all. Children deserve parents who are best suited to raise them, and society has a duty to our children to ensure this happens. By creating tangible ways to treat parenthood as a privilege, like parent certification, we could powerfully execute this duty.

It's time we stop living by a pronatalist assumption that promotes irresponsible reproduction and begin living by one that not just promotes, but demands, responsible reproduction for the benefit of all.

6

THE OFFSPRING
ASSUMPTION

Along with the pronatal assumption that everyone has the right to have children, there has been the related assumption that:

We all have the right to have as many biological children as we want.

Going further than the pronatalist belief that we all have the right to procreate in the first place, this assumption promotes the idea that we can create as many offspring as we choose. Our legal rights today reinforce this as well. Like the right to reproduce, the United States Declaration of Independence's message regarding our right to "life, liberty and the pursuit of happiness" includes our freedom to bring as many children as we want into the world. And as part of our "liberty" in the Fifth Amendment of the U.S. Constitution, we have the right to "marry, establish a home and bring up children"—as many as we want. Neither the government nor anyone else can interfere with our decisions about how many children to have.

The Problem

It may technically be our right, but there's a big problem with the idea that people should be able to have as many children as they want. In the year 2011, we hit seven billion people on the planet and counting. With each child come costs that affect the planet and those already on it. The impact of seven billion and counting in part has to do with our consumption of resources, goods, and space and the consequences of this consumption. The list of what we consume can seem endless. We buy everything that fills our homes. We have cars and buy the oil that fuels them. We heat our homes with coal, oil, or electricity. We use water to wash everything from ourselves to dishes and clothes. We use water to maintain our yards. We buy clothing made of pesticide-grown fabrics and genetically modified foods from supermarkets that ship food in from halfway around the world. We buy gadgets and more gadgets, including the vast array that technology now offers. With every child, the amount of stuff we consume multiplies exponentially. We furnish their rooms, we feed them, we clothe them, we throw out what they outgrow and buy new, and we consume oil driving our children where they need to go. This only hits the tip of the iceberg when it comes to how consumption shoots up with the addition of every person on the planet.

And when it comes to consumption, those in the United States sit at the top of the consumer heap. According to World Bank Development Indicators, the richest 20 percent of the world's population had an almost 77 percent share of the world's private consumption in 2005. By contrast, 60 percent of the world's middle had a 22 percent share of the world's private consumption, and the poorest 20 percent had a 1.5 percent share of the world's private consumption.[1] More recent numbers include the world's richest 20 percent per capita consumption at 86 percent, and the poorest 20 percent at similar levels, at less than two percent.[2] As one of the richest nations in the world, the United States is surely in the highest consumption camp.

Looking at the production of all we consume and the effects of it leads us to the real problems. As Lisa Hymas of Grist.org says, "Without even trying, we Americans slurp up resources from every corner of the globe and then spit 99 percent of them back out again as pollution."[3] The cycle that resources go through from production to disposal or destruction creates carbon emissions into the atmosphere—pollution, that is, and not just a small amount. "Just by virtue of living in America" with its "massive material infrastructure," our carbon footprints far beat all other countries in the world.

A "carbon footprint is a measure of the impact our activities have on the environment, and in particular, climate change. It relates to the amount of greenhouse gases produced in our day-to-day lives through burning fossil fuels for electricity, heating, and transportation, etc. The carbon footprint is a measurement of all greenhouse gases we individually produce and has units of tonnes (or kg) of carbon dioxide equivalent."[4] Typical aspects of a person's carbon footprint include: gas, oil, coal, electricity, private and public transport, air travel, food and drink, clothes, and personal effects. These can be called the "primary" part of each person's footprint. This part is a measure of our direct CO^2 emissions from the burning of fossil fuels, including domestic energy consumption and transportation (e.g., car and plane). We can control our primary footprint. There are secondary aspects of a person's carbon footprint as well. Our secondary footprint is an indirect measure of CO^2 emissions related to the entire life cycle of the products we buy and use, such as the manufacturing of our cars, homes, and furnishings and the share of public services we use. Whether primary or secondary, the bottom line is that "the more we buy, the more emissions will be caused on our behalf."

And Americans' carbon footprints are the highest in the world. According to Datablog at Guardian.uk, the United States is "number one in terms of per capita emissions among the big economies, with 18 tonnes emitted per person." A tonne is a metric ton and equivalent to 1000 kilograms or about 2,200 pounds. So in the standard tons we use in the U.S., that is almost 40,000 pounds or about 20,000 standard tons of carbon emissions *per person*. By comparison, China emits under six tonnes per person and India only 1.38 per person.[5] In addition, the average American generates five times the amount of CO^2 emissions compared to the rest of the world.[6]

Sadly, our carbon footprints are so high that they are at "unsustainable levels."[7] This reality also reflects how the footprints multiply with each incoming generation. Paul A. Murtaugh and Michael G. Schlax of Oregon State University purport that one is "responsible for the carbon emissions of his or her descendants, weighted by their relatedness. That is, a parent is responsible for one-half the emissions of their children, one-quarter the emissions of their grandchildren and so on."[8] In effect, the unsustainability levels multiply with every addition to every generation.

The impact of the human consumption and its collective carbon footprint is degrading the planet's ecosystems. In the past 50 years, "human activity has altered ecosystems faster and more extensively than ever before."[9] This kind of degradation is continuing to jeopardize the earth's "carrying capacity"—meaning just how many people the earth and its resources can continue to sustain or support. The world's current population is consuming at very unsustainable levels. According to World Population Balance, we humans are consuming resources over 50 percent faster than the planet is producing them.[10] David Paxson, President of World Population Balance, says that data from global footprint analyses show that "nearly every country including the United States, is overpopulated relative to its sustainable resource base."[11]

Consider the United States resource use alone for just a moment. If all of the world's people "consumed as much as an average American, it would take the resources of over *five* earths to sustainably support all of them."[12] And this does not factor in the biologically productive land and water needed by other species and what they need from the planet to survive. Paxson indicates that to get the U.S. to long term sustainable resource levels, including maintaining biocapacity for existing humans, their offspring, and other species, the population needs to decline from the current 312 million to *100 million*.[13]

These kinds of numbers point to the real need to reduce human numbers to levels more in line with what our planet can handle. If we don't, and stay on our current course, we will witness even more alarming resource declines and human suffering. It's time to get out from under the pronatalist spell that says we should be able to have as many children as we want. We have reached the point where it's a dangerous mindset to continue to hold. The current world population is already at "two to three times higher than sustainable levels." With the seven billion we've reached, we're already "consuming resources over 50 percent faster than the earth can sustainably produce them."[14] Clearly, considering it all right to bring as many people into the world as we want is making matters worse. It's time to adopt and live by mindsets about reproductive choices that lessen the harm to the planet and all of its living beings.

The Alternative Assumption

Decisions on having children put one's obligation to the planet first.

When it comes to how many children to bring into the world, we've reached a point where we need to first think beyond ourselves. Because we're already overpopulated relative to the earth's limited natural resources, we need to make our first obligation to the planet and those already here, and that means not just humans, but as conservationist Dave Foreman calls them, "wild things" (all other living beings on earth) as well. Our personal desires have to take a back seat, and our sights need to be set on the greater good. And when it comes to that greater good, as David Paxson insightfully puts it, we have to come to terms "with the fact that a person's biological right to have children must be mediated by his or her social responsibility not to have too many."[15] Given the population and the environmental realities we face, what this means is that it's every person's social responsibility to have fewer or no biological children.

Holding and acting on this mindset turns pronatalism on its head, which has to happen in order for us to move in any kind of way toward population stabilization. Instead of adulating the birth of another child, this mindset holds couples who choose to adopt or have one or no biological children in the highest regard. This is because they are doing their part to mitigate the catastrophic impact of a rapidly growing population on resource decline rather than putting what they might personally want first.

Resistance

Many people are going to resist this mindset, because it ultimately means they'll have to truly accept the "impossibility of infinite growth on a finite planet."[16] If we truly accept this, what might it mean? It means facing the fact that we can no longer put ourselves and personal desires first.

In a society that prides itself on freedom and individualism, it can be difficult for people to accept that their personal desires can't always come first. So if people want to keep their own desires as their first priority— e.g., have as many children as they want to have—a state of denial about world realities has to ensue. Denial is a defense mechanism that we can use when we do not want to face a reality—in this case, an overpopulated planet with people gobbling up resources faster than we can replace them. Denial can save us from anxiety or pain, but in this case, it can allow us to continue to do what we want to do at the expense of others and our world. We make ourselves and what we want to do more important, and we look the other way when it comes to being responsible to the planet.

What's another defense mechanism to be able to keep one's own desires as the first priority? Justify one's own behavior by making the reality wrong. In this case, for example, in the United States and other countries with birth rates of about two per woman, it could be easy for people to say that this rate is already low enough such that they don't need to limit their biological births. Although this birth rate level means each person in the couple is replacing themselves, this justification ignores the bigger and more important picture—the resource impact of every child that comes into the world, the serious existing population issues in the world as a whole, and the many children who are already here in need of families and homes.

The motivation to resist the idea that we need to reduce births, making what we want more important, can spring from something that has been of great importance to many people: the desire to continue one's lineage, to create children who will carry on the family name. Today, we are at the place where it's more important to reduce the number of people (thus, the rate we use our resources) than guarantee the continuance of our family lines. Each of us needs to think differently about our lineage and ease our attachment to it. More than ever, making one's family line more important reflects an act of the ego that we can no longer afford. While it has had its historical benefits, e.g., preservation and expansion of assets, having children to ensure that the family name continues is selfish today, especially if we continue to have children until we have a son, which remains the gender that carries on the family name. It's selfish because it reflects doing what we want to do for our own reasons, despite its impact on others and the environment.

Ironically, choosing actions that prioritize the greater good is a lot like the mindset a parent needs to adopt when a child comes on the scene. The mindset and reality is, "It is not about me." As parents, children come first. Similarly, when it comes to our reproductive lives, we have to change our mindset from "me first" to what is in the best interest of the whole.

Less is More

Placing highest value on the idea that "the fewer children, the better" gives new meaning to the saying, "less is more." Let's start with the "more." According to statistician Paul Murtaugh at the University of Oregon, the carbon emissions impact of having one fewer child is almost 20 times greater than the impact of engaging in environmentally friendly practices, such as "driving a high mileage car, recycling, or using energy-efficient appliances and light bulbs" over a lifetime. And when that child has a child of his/her own, and the lineage carries on: "The effect on the environment can be many times the impact produced by a person during their lifetime." Murtaugh reports that every U.S. child "ultimately adds about 9,441 metric tons of carbon dioxide to the carbon legacy of an average parent— about 5.7 times the lifetime emissions for which, on average, a person is responsible."[17] Do the math as the family tree expands, and that's a lot of carbon emissions.

Don't have that child to begin with, and what happens? The carbon emissions stop in their tracks. Have just one? The carbon impact of one is far less than having that next child. The fewer children we have, the greater the positive impact.

Rethinking Only Children

One biological child per couple can make this kind of positive impact. Let's turn our attention beyond the U.S. for a moment. In 2010, Jack Cafferty at CNN cited a study indicating that if every woman had only one child (starting then), the population would decrease (from 6.5 billion then) to 5.5 billion by 2050. If we "do nothing, the population could soar to an unsustainable nine billion during that same time."[18] Looking at the U.S. in particular, in *Maybe One*, author Bill McKibben writes that if we averaged 1.5 children per woman (not the just about two, which is what it is now), and if we reduced immigration somewhat, the U.S. population would be 230 million in 2050, which is what it was when Ronald Reagan was elected.[19] To get to the average of 1.5, more couples would need to have one child, and if they did, it would help us move toward a population with long term sustainable resource levels.

But being an only child is not what is best for the child. It's best for a child to have a sibling, right? Wrong, say McKibben and other experts. The bias against only children began in the late 1800s with psychologist Stanley Hall. He was the Victorian era's "Dr. Spock." He did a study of "peculiar and exceptional children" with 1,045 child subjects. "Peculiar and exceptional" was loosely defined from reasons that were psychological or physical. Forty-six out of the 1,045 (*about 4 percent*) were only children, which, according to him, was a "number entirely out of proportion to children generally." He concluded that an only child is very likely to be peculiar and exceptional. Hall's studies have been criticized for reflecting his own beliefs based on his boyhood experiences, which not so surprisingly included siblings (and lots of them). Even though studies after Hall's largely did not stand up to the rigors of good research, the idea stuck, and the conventional wisdom to this day has been that it is not good to have an only child.[20]

Better studies to date say otherwise. Toni Falbo, a professor of educational psychology and sociology at the University of Texas at Austin, and her colleague Denise Polit looked at past studies more closely. They analyzed 115 studies of only children in the U.S. across class and race from 1925 onward. The studies looked at adjustment, character, sociability, achievement, and intelligence variables. They found that only children "aren't measurably different from other kids" except that they, "along with firstborns and people who have only one sibling, score higher in measures of intelligence and achievement." They are no more likely to be lonely, shy, unpopular, selfish, or maladjusted than children with siblings. They also analyzed personality studies and found that the "personalities of only children were indistinguishable from their peers with siblings."[21] No published research can demonstrate any truth behind the stereotypes. On the flip side, only children experience some benefits that those with siblings do not get to experience: No sibling rivalry, which can have an impact on a person's life, and no "differential affection," meaning that they do not have to compete for their parents' attention.

These truths about only children need to become more widespread to remove people's reluctance to consider having only one biological child. They need to see it isn't only all right to have one child, but it is also doing right by that child. As McKibben argues, more single-child families are necessary so that they and their parents will be more likely to live in a sustainable world.

Parents who want to have more than one biological child need to look harder at why this is the case. Is it because they didn't get the gender one or both parents wanted with first one? Or because they want a boy *and* a girl? Now more than ever, it is important for those who think they want more than one child to answer what need are they filling for *themselves,* and why they would put themselves and what they want first, knowing the impact of bringing another child into the world. It's also important for those who think they want more than one child to ask themselves if their need could be filled in a way other than bringing a second biological child onto the planet. For example, how about filling that need by parenting a child who is already here?

Rethinking Adoption

When it comes to being a parent, it has been all too common to think that "biological is best." Now more than ever, we need to value the opportunity to become a parent to children who are already here. Dina McQueen, author of *Finding Aster: Our Ethiopian Adoption Story,* reframes it best: We need to shift our mindset to see adoption "as the first choice, not the last option."[22]

Why is it so common to see it as the last option? Because pronatalist dogma has stressed that having your *own* child is *the* way to have a child. The idea that having a biological child is somehow better is a myth that we can no longer afford. One reason people have commonly believed that it's best to have "your own" is because they think they won't be able to love their adopted child like they would love their own biological child. According to the Hope for Orphans organization, this just isn't the case. Parents may have this concern, but research tells us something different: 95 percent of adoptive parents say they experience a strong attachment to their child.[23]

In addition to this myth, there are others about adoption itself. One myth is that there aren't many healthy babies available for adoption in the United States. Adoption expert Mardie Caldwell thinks differently. Twenty-five years ago, she founded the Lifetime Adoption Center and has helped thousands of families adopt. In reality, she says, there are "tens of thousands of families each year that adopt healthy, newborn babies through adoption." Many of them are through open adoption, where the biological mother, often called the birth mother, may have chosen the family herself.[24]

Many people also don't look at adoption seriously because they assume it just plain costs too much. Hope for Orphans says that the cost ranges from "nothing upwards of $30,000." Now, that is a lot of money. However, what many people don't realize is how much assistance is available for parents who adopt. There are federal adoption tax credits and grants for sizeable amounts to assist families wanting to adopt. There are also fee reductions for special needs children, and financial assistance is often offered through churches. The way Hope for Orphans sees it, adoption can be made "affordable for almost anyone willing to pursue the options available."[25]

There are also myths about the process, adoptive parents' rights, and the children themselves. While it has been common to believe that it takes a long time to complete the adoption process, recent polls indicate otherwise; according to Caldwell, the process generally takes about a year.[26] Some would-be adoptive parents also have concerns that the child's birth parents would be able to take the child back. Today's adoption laws protect against that if the laws are followed. Hope for Orphans suggests that adoptive parents work with attorneys who have expertise in this area and can make sure all legal papers are signed. This will "nearly eliminate this possibility."[27]

When it comes to the children themselves, many people believe that there are too many babies available for adoption who have been "drug-exposed." Caldwell clarifies that "most women considering adoption for their children are not using drugs." The majority are "leading relatively healthy lives and even seeking ongoing prenatal care."[28] And many others worry that adopted children probably have more emotional issues than would their biological children. It is true that some children who have had traumatic experiences prior to adoption may have an increased chance of emotional and behavioral issues. However, Hope for Orphans makes the very real point that *any* child may encounter emotional and behavioral issues.[29] The truth is that having biological children does not guarantee they will be any "easier" than adopted children.

It's time to take serious heed of Caldwell's advice: "Maybe if a woman deeply feels the desire to give birth, she will do it one time, then decide that adopting to grow her family is the most conscious choice to make."[30] Even better, decide that giving birth is not as important as parenting children already here who need homes and lots of love. If more people decided to take the "win-win" that adoption provides—the parents get the experience of parenthood and adopted children find parents to raise them—the world could be saved from the carbon wake that comes with every child.

If we see adoption more as the preferred choice, it will also help women who want to give birth but are having a hard time conceiving. Rather than feel something is "wrong" and that the only solution is an expensive procedure like in vitro fertilization, they could more readily decide to put that money toward adopting a child. They would be less likely to feel the need to have a biological child to fulfill the desire to be a parent.

We're at a point where we need to loosen our value on biological over adoptive children. Instead of thinking only of ourselves and the ego gratification we might get from having "our own" children, we need to do the right thing for the planet and those already on it. When those who want to be parents think beyond themselves and adopt, benefits accrue to those parents, their adopted children, and the world.

Rethinking What's Selfish

When it comes to accepting the choice to have no children, we've come a long way in the last few generations. Because of pronatalism, not having children by choice has been perceived as selfish. Our perception of what it means to be selfish needs to change. Society needs to view the refusal to put the planet and all beings on it first as the selfish choice. The reverence needs to go to those who are not contributing to population growth and the problems that go along with it.

Rethinking Incentives

One powerful way to demonstrate regard for those choosing to act on behalf of the greater good is to reward those actions. In this country, our government has been doing just the opposite in the form of child tax credits. This needs to change. Instead of creating tax policies that encourage the birth of children, the government needs to provide incentives to *reduce* the number of births.

As David Paxson points out, however, we won't see lawmakers attempting to change these kinds of laws unless people first accept the reality that resources are finite and too many people are using them too fast.[31] In this regard, government tax credits in the form of cash encourage people to look the other way. Encouraging people to have more biological children continues to push a set of beliefs that allows business and political power structures to ensure their survival and power. And to keep that power, these factions need the engine called capitalism, which drives the unending practice of consumption. From the perspective of capitalism, there are never too many consumers. However, this is shortsighted in an age when we're out-consuming our resources. The reality is that there are plenty of people here to keep the consumerist engines running. In fact, there are too many.

We need to stop drinking the pronatalist Kool-Aid that says "the more children the better," and make sure our lawmakers know we no longer believe it's in our country's best interest, nor the world's best interest for that matter. One way to move toward practices that would be in everyone's best interest is to push our lawmakers to reverse the child credit incentive structure. For example, federal and state tax law should expand the benefits to those who adopt. In an addition to federal tax credits, adoptive parents should continue to receive an exemption for each adopted child, but one that's significantly larger than what biological parents get. Those who have no children should be able to take an exemption, although not as large as adoptive parents. Those parents with one biological child should receive a nominal exemption. Parents with two children should receive no exemption, and parents with more than two biological children should be penalized an amount that would create enough incentive for them to not have that third child in the first place.

How about also considering a "parent carbon tax?" While not in effect to date, the idea of a "carbon tax" on the carbon content of fossil fuels has been out there as a way to incentivize businesses and households to reduce their carbon emissions. According to Carbontax.org, it operates from the overarching idea "that the most effective way to reduce a 'negative externality' is to tax it."[32] A "parent carbon tax" could be designed with the same idea. The thousands of tons of carbon emissions that are associated with every child parents bring into the world certainly qualify as a "negative externality." Similarly, adoptive parents and non-parents would not be subject to the parent carbon tax, but biological parents would. And with each additional child, this tax would increase as a way to discourage the conception of more children.

Rethinking Humanitarianism & Patriotism

Yes, bearing children still remains a right under this country's constitution. But the pronatalist assumption that we can have as many children as we want harms society and our natural environment. Given the impact of population growth on resource decline and degradation in today's world, when it comes to our reproduction, we have an important social responsibility to that world. Each person's existence has an environmental impact, which affects humans and other species. It's up to us to choose reproductive action that lessens this impact.

Some people might say that even if valuing a mindset of "the fewer the better" results in the reduction of births, getting it to Paxson's 100 million number in the U.S. is just not possible; we've already gone far beyond the possibility of a sustainable population. Some say this is true of the world as well. If the world averaged closer to a birth rate of one child per woman, the population *might* stop at eight billion before it begins to decrease, and that number is still way past a sustainable population.

Even if this is the case, we owe it to the generations already here and those in the future (and all other beings on the planet other than human beings) to think beyond ourselves and do what we can to mitigate the population and natural resource problems that exist today. We have an obligation to leave future generations as healthy a planet as possible. And the most powerful thing we can do to this end is reduce our reproduction. Seen in this way, having fewer offspring is not the selfish, but the selfless, act. Having fewer, not more, biological offspring is the true humanitarian act because it ultimately lessens the suffering of people and the world's natural environment.[33] While we may have the legal right to produce any number of offspring, we have the ability to choose to put the country's or the world's best interests ahead of self-interest. When we choose not to have children or to limit the number we do have because we're mindful of the impact of each child on the planet's resources, we show deep loyalty not only to our own country, but to the future of the world at large.

7

THE FULFILLMENT
ASSUMPTION

Pronatalism has long told us that children are what bring true meaning to our lives. From that perspective, parenthood answers life's ultimate existential questions about life purpose and our reason for living. The pronatalist assumption has been:

The ultimate path to fulfillment in life is parenthood.

In other words, the assumption is that until we become parents, we don't know what purpose, meaning, or fulfillment really means. We may have successful careers, and do many other things in life, but becoming a mother and father is what makes life truly worthwhile. Those who don't have children either by choice or circumstance are seen as missing out on the opportunity to find out what life is really about— raising children.

How It Came To Be

The origins of this assumption are not difficult to trace. In the past, when medicine was less advanced, there were greater risks associated with both pregnancy and childbirth. Romanticized myths about pregnancy and motherhood were needed to ensure the continued survival of the family, says sociologist E.E. LeMasters. Feminist Leta Hollingsworth called these romanticized myths "illusions" and saw them as a means of social control to manipulate people to have children.[1] The myth was emphasized, while the negatives, such as difficulties during pregnancy and childbirth, death in childbirth, or the downsides of childrearing, were not mentioned. And one of the biggest positive messages given for the mother and father was that parenthood would bring them the ultimate fulfillment in life.

That was then—when having children was more of a necessity. Why has this kind of glorification continued when this is no longer the case and, in fact, detrimental to us all? Because powerful societal structures, such as our governments, corporations, and religious organizations have a major stake in continuing to glorify the fulfillment that comes with parenthood and children. While the population no longer needs to continue increasing as in times past, governmental, corporate, and religious factions need to keep the population increasing to maintain and grow their power. It's in their best interest to keep the population rising; the more people there are, the more taxpayers, the more products and services to sell, and the more members to contribute to the Church's power and wealth. Perpetuating the idea that parenthood is an experience you have to have in life to be truly fulfilled means more children, which ultimately serves to make these entities even more powerful.

Today, the infertility industry takes this line of thinking further. Its very existence is founded on the idea that we should be willing to do just about anything to have our own kids in order to have an amazing life. If we "can't" have children, we won't have that amazing life, our lives will never be "complete," and we'll feel like we somehow "failed." This kind of messaging has made the infertility business soar. As this technology continues to advance, the more procedures we see that reinforce these messages. For example, take "oocyte cryopreservation" or egg freezing. Technology now offers women a "realistic chance to extend their fertility."[2] A woman can spend at least $15,000 to "produce as many eggs as science can help her produce and keep them in a cryogenic vat indefinitely." On one hand, we might say this is a good thing, as it gives women even more power to choose when they are going to become mothers. However, it still puts having a child front and center as the thing to do to make life complete—now, no matter the woman's age or how long her body can withstand a pregnancy. You can now embark on this ultimate experience at virtually any age. With hormone treatments, some postmenopausal women can carry a child until the age of 60.[3] Our fixation on having to experience motherhood has now reached a point where we have to ask when it's too old to become a mother—50? 60? Older? Pronatalism would say never!

Beyond the fact that pronatal messages have made people believe that raising children will bring them fulfillment in life, the truth is that many people *do* find meaning in their lives by having children. Raising them gives people a clear purpose and can be a very fulfilling experience. This is a good thing. The more the parents love the parenting process, the better it is for the children.

However, as many parents will attest, parenthood is not all a bed of roses. This is where the romanticized myths step back in. Even though there are many things about parenthood that don't match the romanticized version portrayed by pronatalism, we're not supposed to mess with the message machine that says it's the greatest thing that ever happened to us. There are strong taboos about describing the experience of parenthood in any kind of negative way. Why? By not doing so, the romanticized version of parenthood gets to stay firmly in place, and people will continue to want to become parents.

Rufus Griscom and Alisa Volkman, creators of the parenting site, Babble.com, have talked about some of the taboos of parenting.[4] One taboo involves miscarriage. We are not supposed to talk about this if it happens to us. We also can't say we didn't fall in love with our baby the moment we saw it because we're supposed to fall in love immediately. We're also not supposed to talk about how lonely day-to-day life as a primary caregiver can be or that our happiness has declined since becoming a parent. We're supposed to say our life has never been better, so rich and full. Making these kinds of true but negative statements is taboo because they reveal difficulties and challenges. We're not ever supposed to question whether parenthood is truly fulfilling us. At least that is what pronatalism tells us. According to its doctrine, of course, parenthood is fulfilling us.

But is it? Wray Herbert, author of *On Second Thought: Outsmarting Your Mind's Hard-Wired Habits*, tells us that "study after study has shown that parents, compared to adults without kids, experience lower emotional well-being—fewer positive feelings and more negative ones—and have unhappier marriages and suffer more from depression. Yet many of these same parents continue to insist that their children are an essential source of happiness—indeed that a life without children is a life unfulfilled."[5] What's going on here? A psychological phenomenon called "cognitive dissonance." It's when parents need to subscribe to the "myth of parental joy because otherwise [they] would have a hard time justifying the huge investment that kids require" (and all the other negatives).

Research supports the idea that cognitive dissonance can be at play when it comes to idealizing the parenthood experience. For example, researchers Richard Eibach and Steven Mock conducted a study that looked at the high costs of raising kids and parents' predictions of leisure time with them.[6] When parents had the high costs of children in mind, they were much more likely to say that they enjoyed spending time with their children, and they also anticipated spending more leisure time with their kids. When they were aware of parenthood's price tag, they created an idealized image of their family life, in this case having to do with leisure time spent with their children. Eibach and Mock found that the high costs of raising children influenced parents to idealize the emotional rewards of having children. This supported their hypothesis that parenthood idealization functions to rationalize parental investments.

The ability to rationalize like this helps keep the old assumption about parenthood and fulfillment in place. Instead of looking at the downsides of parenthood—which might make us question if it has truly brought the meaning and fulfillment we thought it would to our lives—we find things to believe that justify our (in this case irreversible) choices.

The Truth

Raising children may give purpose or a solid direction to one's life, but is it necessarily a purpose that every person wants? Similarly, raising children may give our lives a sense of meaning, so it's hard not to see it as a meaningful endeavor. However, the question for each person is—will this meaningful endeavor truly bring what fulfillment in life means *to me*?

Discovering what brings meaning, personally, can be a challenging endeavor. Many people just don't know the answer for themselves, so they end up doing what society tells them and what they see others doing to find meaning. For many people, the answer is found in the experience of parenthood. But it isn't so for others.

Dr. Phil's survey of over 20,000 parents, in which one third said they would not do it over again if they had the chance, speaks volumes.[7] This sentiment is particularly well-expressed by this father from the blog, Motherlode: Adventures in Parenting:

"My wife and I didn't get married until we were in our 30s, and didn't have our first child until five years after that. We were both well-educated, with great jobs, and we lived a jet-set lifestyle: apartment downtown, busy jobs, etc. We now have two kids, ages 4 and 1. No matter how well prepared I thought I was, I was not prepared for the sheer magnitude of changes to my life. Being the go-to guy at work, who can jump on a plane at a moment's notice to go meet a client: gone. Working on my master's degree with evening classes: gone. Playing on a local basketball league: gone. Playing golf on Saturdays and lazy Sunday mornings: gone. Living in a bohemian loft apartment: nope, now it's a house in the suburbs with a 45-minute commute. No more personal projects, like the book I wanted to write, or starting a consulting business on the side, or training to run a marathon: all gone. So if I knew then what I know now, I might have only had one child, or zero.... I have committed myself to being the best darn father I can be, and I have slowly accepted the fact that all those personal dreams are basically pushed to the side because of that."[8]

Others read candid writings like this and are inspired to share what's true for them, as this woman does:

"I am one of the taboo. I have children and many regrets. My life is ALL about my children. I have dedicated my life to being the best mother possible, because my children deserve to have the best mother possible. It was not THEIR choice to be born. But, I would have done it differently if I had thought about it consciously. It wasn't a conscious decision to have or not have children. I wish I had put more thought into the decision. My 11-year-old daughter has stated many, many times that she does not want to have children. I have never once discouraged her from that choice. My mother has, but I talked to her about it and she hasn't said anything since. My mother has never stated it, but I believe she has regrets about having children. I'm glad I was born, but I believe every child should be a wanted child. Kids turn out better when their parents are happy. Even if the parents really truly love their children, as I love mine, and I know my mom loves me. But I cannot say either one of us is truly happy."[9]

There are lots of stories like this about parental regret. While there are many parents without regrets, there are many who resonate with these parents' feelings. Why might so many parents find that parenthood is not all it's cracked up to be? One reason is that the day-to-day reality does not match the romanticized version of parenthood.

Researcher Daniel Kahneman, a Nobel Prize-winning behavioral economist, surveyed over 900 working women and found that childcare ranked 16th in "pleasurability" out of 19 activities.[10] Childcare ranked below activities such as preparing food, watching TV, exercising, talking on the phone, napping, shopping, and even doing housework. For many parents, the activities that are part of the reality of child rearing don't always add up to the experience of fulfillment.

New York Times Magazine contributing editor, Jennifer Senior, suggests another reason why the act of parenting may not be all it's cracked up to be for many parents. Maybe it's because the "experience of raising children has fundamentally changed."[11] According to *Psychology Today*, an over-focus on kids can explain a large part of why parents might not experience profound satisfaction from the parenting process.[12] In fact, survey research with over 13,000 respondents by Robin Simon of Wake Forest University indicates that the discontent goes further; adults with children, regardless of race, class, or gender, experience depression and unhappiness in greater numbers than non-parents.[13] She believes this is partly due to the "anticipation of the overflow of bliss" that comes with having children. "Our expectations that children guarantee a life filled with happiness, joy, excitement, contentment, satisfaction, and pride" often just don't end up matching the reality. And according to San Diego State researcher Jean Twenge, the most dissatisfaction can be experienced by the women who wait longer and longer to have children.[14] The idealistic expectation that it's going to be the most fulfilling experience butts up against the realities of parenting along with more memories of what life was like before having children. As Twenge says, because you were a non-parent longer, "You know what you're missing."

Now, the truth is that many parents may know what they are missing but find that parenthood brings them purpose, meaning, and fulfillment nonetheless. Many parents talk about the profound feelings of satisfaction and reward when they have special "transcendent" moments with their children, and many feel the same when they look back at the experience as a whole. But do the special moments with their children or the hindsight feelings about parenthood equate to a deep purpose in life—a life rich in meaning? For some, the answer is yes, and for others, the answer is a clear no. Because the reality is that it isn't true for everyone, we need to abandon the pronatalist mindset and adopt an alternative one that expands a purposeful, meaningful, and fulfilling life beyond parenthood.

The Alternative Assumption

Parenthood is one path to purpose and fulfillment in life.

This Alternative Assumption reflects the reality that parenthood is not what makes every person's life feel complete. It is merely one path in life. When we adopt this idea, people will feel freer to find what purpose uniquely means to them and not to feel that no matter what that is, parenthood "has" to be part of it. Finding what purpose means to each of us and honoring that purpose is a journey we all take in life. Although we share the same need for meaning, we all differ in what it takes to fulfill it.

What does finding purpose and meaning really mean? As the book *Finding Fulfillment From the Inside Out* puts forth, we don't find what purpose means to us by just doing what others around us are doing. We ultimately don't find what it means by copying others' lives, living out the unlived lives of others, being driven by materialism, or by chasing goals for the goal's sake. People commonly think it means discovering what they love to do and making it their vocation or avocation. However, finding a deep sense of purpose is much more than that. It starts with finding our "core curiosities."[15] The famous scientist Linus Pauling once said, "Satisfaction of one's curiosity is one of the greatest sources of happiness in life." Our curiosities are our interests—things we are drawn to and enjoy doing. Our "core" curiosities are those things that give us a kind of pleasure that feels deeper than usual, more intense, and more sustained. Core curiosities can feel insatiable and deeply move us when we engage in them.

To get at our core curiosities, we can ask ourselves these kinds of questions: What were my obsessions or preoccupations as a child? What do I have a deep reverence for? What fascinates me or fills me with awe? What do I adore or admire? What captivates me? What things do I get easily immersed in? Once we know our core curiosities, we have to figure out why these core curiosities move us so and discern exactly what it is about them that fills us. It means looking beyond the interest itself to something deeper. At the root of each of our core curiosities is something our inmost selves want to experience by engaging in that core curiosity.

Let's take the example of parenting as a core curiosity. To get at what is really filling us means asking what experience(s) we are looking for *through* the act of parenting. The inner experience we seek could be a deep connection with another human being. It could be the experience of guiding or mentoring. It could be the experience of unconditional love. The deeper, inner experiences from parenting can be many things and will be different for different people. And when we make our lives about having those deeper, inner experiences, we'll feel a deep sense of inner purpose because we are being filled from the inside out.

However, what is too often not realized is that there's not just one way to have the inner experiences we long for. For example, parenting is not the *only* way to experience a deep connection with another person, nor is it the *only* way to experience guiding or mentoring, or unconditional love. There are many other ways to experience these things. Part of finding what gives us deep purpose means not only uncovering one's core curiosities and the inner experiences we're looking for, but also figuring out the right "doing" to get those experiences. Is it parenting? Is it working with kids who are not our own in ways that require intense connection with them? Is it playing an influential role in a child's life—and if so, at what age of the child's life? Figuring this out is akin to figuring out how we want to use our parent competencies. We have to figure this out and then choose the best "strategies" that will give us the inner experiences we long for, which will fill us from within.

Take another example—the story of Chris. As an architect, he loves the aspect of his work that involves innovations in structural design. He also avidly reads sci-fi novels and watches sci-fi movies. He loves to travel to exotic places. He collects vintage ties seriously. Classic cars also fascinate him; he works on them and goes to lots of car shows. Chris figured out that behind sci-fi and exotic travel is his desire to experience the unconventional. Behind marveling at classic cars and innovative architecture is the experience of understanding the extraordinary. Vintage ties reflect his adoration of what is rare and uncommon. If he makes his life about having experiences where he can encounter the unconventional, the extraordinary, and the rare, it will fill him from the inside out. He boils it down to its essence by expressing his purpose as, "I live to encounter the uncommon." He got to the essence of the experiences he was looking for by starting with his core curiosities, but they are not the only ways for a person to experience the extraordinary or rare. It's how Chris experiences it. For others, the purpose might be similar, but they might fill that purpose through other things having nothing to do with sci-fi, cars, or architecture.

When we know the experiential themes behind our most intense interests, we know what our deeper selves seek to experience in life. When we know these things about ourselves, we know the core of our *inner* purpose. In a nutshell, finding purpose and meaning means knowing the answer to this question: What does my inner most self seek to experience? And the answer to this question is different for everyone.

Unlike the script we are told to follow—go to college, get a job, get married, have children—we each have our unique path to follow so that we can find what purpose and meaning are for us. Parenthood can be the means by which we get to have the experiences our innermost self yearns for; however, it may not be the only forum or even the best forum, for that matter, given our life aspirations and goals. This is why it's important to know what purpose means to us *before* we have children. We need to know more about what gives us a rich sense of meaning in life first, and then determine how raising children will fit into this picture—or not. If we have not figured out what inner purpose means, and we're contemplating having a child, it is critical to ask what experiences we think we want through having a child *and* if parenthood is the only way to have these experiences. With an irreversible decision like parenthood, it's important to discern these answers carefully before choosing whether or not to have children.

Although pronatalism has told us that parenthood is the ticket to a full life, people with no children by choice show us that there are many paths to purpose, meaning, and fulfillment. Adopting a new assumption that makes the "natal" piece optional for a purposeful life increases the chances that more people will not have romanticized notions about parenthood as the key to fulfillment. They will then not become parents and realize they made a mistake. It will also allow people to widen their quest for what purpose means to them and live their lives in honor of that quest. As a result, there will be more people who will live lives rich in what purpose and meaning uniquely means to them.

8

THE ELDERHOOD ASSUMPTION

One of the most common things people ask the childfree is, "Who is going to be there for you when you are old?" Why do they ask this question? Because they're operating under the old pronatalist assumption that:

My children will be there for me when I am old.

Pronatalism tells us that one of the many benefits of having children is the assurance that they will take care of us in our later years. We go through all of the hard work to raise our children so that down the road, they will be there for us when we're old. Part of the parenthood agreement from one generation to the next as the older generation ages is, "I raised you; now it's your turn to help me."

In times past, families lived with or near each other. Also in times past, they needed to stick together to survive. However, families in today's times look very different. Family members often live far apart from each other and have their own lives. The expectation that our children will be there for us remains strong, is even seen as a given, but is it really true today?

Today's Many Faces of "Being There"

Today, there are 311 million people in the U.S.[1] According to 2009 figures, 13 percent, or about 40 million of this population, are

65 or older.[2] What are the living situations of this age group? Many of them live on their own—with their spouse or alone. In 2008, 29 percent of all people 65 years and older lived alone.[3] According to a 2010 report by the Federal Interagency Forum on Aged-Related Statistics (Forum), 72 percent of men aged 65 and over lived with their spouse, 19 percent lived alone, 7 percent lived with one of their children or other family members, and 3 percent lived with non-relatives. Forty-two percent of women aged 65 and over lived with their spouse, 40 percent lived alone, 17 percent lived with one of their children or other family members, and 2 percent lived with non-relatives.[4] This generation of older people is living longer than ever before. According to Elena Portacolone, a researcher on the aged, "Thanks to the 'longevity revolution' and to the desire to live at home, the share of adults living alone is destined to increase."[5]

Others over the age of 65 live in assisted living or retirement community environments. According to the National Center for Assisted Living (NCAL), about one million seniors were living in assisted living environments in 2008.[6] According to geriatrician and founder of the Eden Alternative and Green House Project, Dr. Bill Thomas, we have "more nursing homes (16,100) than Starbucks coffee shops" in this country, and "nearly 1.6 million people live in these nursing homes."[7]

If children live near their parents, it increases the chances they will help their parents and "do for them" in a myriad of ways, including assisting with domestic matters, health care, finances, and insurance matters. However, these days, life situations very often mean adult children don't live near their parents. With extended families more spread out, adult children often cannot be there for their parents when it's crucial. They can go stay with their parents for a period of time when the parents are dealing with health issues, for example, or very commonly these days, adult children can take charge when it's time for their parents or a surviving parent to receive home help or in-home care. They can also assist when it's time to find an assisted living facility or nursing home, although the parents may not always feel like this kind of support is "being there for them" if they don't want to leave their home. From afar, adult children can also tend to coordinative and administrative matters that come up when parents are living in assisted living facilities and nursing homes.

Financial assistance is another way adult children can be there for their parents in their later years. This help can take many forms, such as helping parents with the costs of living, health care, home help services, assisted living, or nursing home care. Such financial help may not be a small matter. According to a recent Forum report, seniors 65 and over report that housing costs account for 35-38 percent of their annual expenditures; health care, 12-14 percent; and transportation, 14-15 percent. Thirty-seven percent of those in this age group report "housing cost burdens." Seniors report paying almost $16,000 a year in health care costs, and almost all, some 95 percent, report having out-of-pocket costs for health care services.[8]

Housing costs can also be financially problematic for many seniors. According to the MetLife Mature Market Institute reports, the average annual cost for a semiprivate room in a nursing home is nearly $67,000, and in certain parts of the country, it's much higher.[9] While Medicaid will step in and pay for nursing home care if seniors financially qualify and have little or no assets, this is not the case with other types of long term care. Except in rare cases, Medicaid doesn't cover assisted living or home-based health care. That means if the parents don't have the funds, their children often have to pay those costs. According to the MetLife Mature Market Institute, the average cost for an assisted living facility in 2006 was $35,616 a year, and the average cost for a home health aide was $19 an hour.[10]

Like in times past, the expectation that children will be there for their parents as they age remains strong. And while it takes different forms today, more often than not, adult children *do* want to be there for their parents in any way they can. This is a good thing. But as many parents know, it doesn't always work out this way. Their children often live far away, and/or they have professional or personal responsibilities to their immediate nuclear family that make it difficult for them to be there for their parents in the ways the parents need or expect it. The belief that adult children will unquestionably be there for their parents needs a harder look. Given the realities of society today, the mindset may need to change from the parents' belief that, "I raised you; now it's your turn to help me" to the adult children's position that, "You raised me; now I will help you if/how I can."

Is It Wise to Bank on It?

In my book, *Families of Two*, a childfree woman named Amy speaks to the assumption that our children will be there for us. When asked what she was going to do when she was 70 with no children there for her, she said, "Just because you have children does not mean they are going to take care of you. It doesn't even mean they are going to like you!"[11]

What larger point is Amy making? That there are no guarantees in life. We may expect that our children will indeed be there for us, but that does not ensure that they will be.

The truth is that parents may want to live independently and want their adult children to live near them so that they can provide them with assistance when they need it, but adult children may not want to do this. More commonly today, adult children and their families don't live near their parents or siblings. They may be able to assist their parents from afar, but if that's not enough, the parents may very well need to find other ways to get the support they need.

There's also no guarantee adult children will have the financial means to assist their parents. The parents may have saved all of their lives but are now living longer, so the savings just aren't enough. According to elder researcher Elena Portacolone, there's a big catch-22 for many seniors. The majority of seniors are not the ones who qualify for government services. The majority are also not the ones who have the financial capacity to provide for their own care. The majority are somewhere in between—they are not poor enough to qualify for government-sponsored services but don't have enough financial capability to provide for their own care.[12] Being in this financial position, they often need to turn to their children for assistance. But the adult children may not have the capability to financially help their parents with everything from living expenses, home help, in-home care needs, and assisted living or nursing home expenses.

Many adult children these days don't have the means but somehow take on the financial squeeze anyway. According to research conducted by Pew Research Center, "thirty percent of adult children in the United States contribute financially to their parents' care."[13] Too often, they do so to their own long term detriment. While the adult children spend large amounts of money on their parents, they often ignore their own savings and retirement accounts. Or they may not even have a savings account at all. Almost 30 percent of Americans report not having saved for retirement—not one dollar.[14] By trying to take care of their parents, they can go into debt. This situation can set up a recurring cycle—adult children jeopardize their own finances, thus risking that they will put their children in the same position in the years to come.

Then, there is the other 70 percent who don't contribute to their parents' care whether they can afford it or not. Granted, some elderly do not need financial assistance. Others, however, may have adult children who do have the means but choose not to assist their parents in this regard.

There is also no guarantee adult children will have the ability to house their parent(s), or that they will even want their parents to live with them. And even if they do want their parent (s) to live with them, it can be a challenge and take a toll on the adult children. In addition to the financial challenge, caregiving responsibilities can be stressful and overwhelming. It can be physically and emotionally difficult. It can also affect the adult children's work life, raising absenteeism or causing workday interruptions because of the need to tend to matters related to the parent(s). If there is enough disruptive work time, it may even threaten their jobs. A study by MetLife estimates that U.S. businesses incur costs as high as $33 billion per year from the decreased productivity of working caregivers.[15]

When adult children have their elder parent(s) living with them and it gets to be too much, terrible things can happen. There are many stories about families abandoning their elder parent or relatives who had been living with them by leaving them in a public place or a hospital doorstep. This is known as "granny dumping." Many times, the adult child caregivers do something crazy like this when they need a break from the caregiving, which can be very demanding when the parent or relative has Alzheimer's or a very challenging health issue, and they don't know what else to do. With the "granny dump," they get a much needed break, and the elder person does end up back home with them. Or in other cases, it's the first step to finding another caregiving situation.

"Granny dumping" often happens when there are insufficient respite care programs. Respite programs provide planned short-term and time-limited breaks for families (and other unpaid caregivers) as a way to support the caregiving relationship. In 2006, the United States Congress passed the Lifespan Respite Care Act, which is intended to make respite care more accessible nationally. When it isn't, like in Australia, "granny dumping" can be more of a "common phenomenon." Geriatric Services Director Nick Brennan says you see more "terrible stories about people who have clearly used the hospital system and emergency services to sort out their unwanted problem."[16]

Even if this sort of awful thing never happens, elders living with one of their children can bring other surprises their adult children might not expect. Parents of adult children who live with their kids can end up caring for their children's children. Census figures have indicated that about 42 percent of co-resident grandparents have primary care responsibilities for grandchildren under age 18, and 39 percent of co-resident grandparents have cared for their grandchildren for five years or more.[17] While some grandparents may like and want this role, it can often be too much for them. For others, caring for their children's children in exchange for receiving their children's support may not be what they expected or necessarily wanted.

Unexpected outcomes are always a possibility for the elderly, many of whom do not expect to end up in a nursing home. A La Vie Childfree blog survey respondent and nursing home professional has observed that 90 percent of the elderly in nursing homes have adult children. She asks if kids are supposed to be there for you when you're old, why are there so many people in nursing homes to begin with? The parents may not want to be in this living situation, but this may be what works best for the adult children, not necessarily their parents.

Whether the parents are in nursing homes, assisted living communities, or even living on their own, being there can just mean visiting them. The odds are not what *Families of Two*'s Amy said—that the adult children don't like their parents. So often the adult children do like their parents, but the fact is that they don't want to be with their parents as much as their parents want to be with them. Research tells us that elder parents can often have smaller social networks and lead less active social lives than their peers without children.[18] This seems to suggest that the parents' social spheres can revolve more around their children and their families. This is wonderful, as long as this social sphere is active. But often, it may not be as active as the parent(s) would like. Other studies indicate that marriage, not parenthood, makes the difference when it comes to elders feeling they have a strong support network.[19] They feel their spouse is more at the heart of their support network than their kids.

While our children may indeed be there for us when we are old, the reality is that it may be unwise to assume it will happen the way we think or hope. Too many things can turn out in a way that we don't expect. When it comes to the support from adult children, the odds of things turning out differently than we thought are higher today than most people would think.

Is It Fair to Expect It?

For a long time, people have been taught that it's a child's duty and obligation to take care of his or her parents when they are old. However, it's worth asking whether this is a fair expectation. Shoshana, who was interviewed in *Families of Two*, asks this question: "Is it fair to say to a kid, 'I brought you into this world so you can one day take care of me?'"[20] When someone expects their children to be there for them when they are old, who are they ultimately thinking of? Themselves. This puts what the parents want and expect before what might ultimately be best for their adult children. If we put the focus on adult children first, the parents would be more apt to ask themselves: Is it fair to expect my kids to live near me so they can assist me when I need help? Is it fair to ask them to assist me when the time off work could negatively affect or even jeopardize their job? Is it fair to expect them to help me financially when it's a financial burden on them? Is it fair to expect them to help me do whatever it takes—to give me their time, financial resources, etc., so that I can continue to live in my home? Is it fair to expect them to come to see me as much as I want if that's not what works best for them and their lives?

Many parents do ask themselves these questions, but many do it too late. If parents asked themselves these kinds of questions earlier in their lives instead of expecting without question that their kids will take care of them, it could prompt them to do more advanced planning for their later years. Instead of relying on their expectations, parents can take more responsibility for their later years before they get there. This can end up not only working in their best interests, but in the best interests of their adult children as well.

The Alternative Assumption

Finding my elderhood support structure is my responsibility.

The first concept worth examining in this Alternative Assumption is the notion of "elderhood." Dr. Bill Thomas coined this term as a stage of life beyond the adulthood stage of our lives. It is our final phase of life and should be valued for what it can be—"rich … deep … and meaningful."[21] Thomas believes that the flaw in our human condition is not the biology of aging but "the way our culture views the structure of the life cycle." The notion that we're of more value when we are older only if we can still look, feel, and act the way we did when we were younger only serves to work against us in our later years. We resist, rather than welcome, elderhood with an open embrace. Rather than striving for "everlasting youthful adulthood," we can approach this time in our lives in a way that honors our elderhood.

If we honor elderhood and ourselves in it, we can more easily do what this assumption also does—turn the focus of the expectations away from others and on to ourselves. It places value on developing one's support structure and does not assume it will be there automatically through blood relatives. It advocates support but without expectations about that support.

This Alternative Assumption does not advocate that responsibility means that we must remain "independent" no matter what until we die. This has been a popular position in our society. As elder researcher Elena Portocolone puts it, "We live in an individualistic society … that rewards self-sufficiency," and we "have a duty to be free, self-reliant and independent." Our society tends to think that feeling independent enhances the quality of life because it "increases a perception of being in control and not intruding on others."[22] Ironically, there's the expectation that children will be there for their parents when they are old, but many, when they get there, will push that help away because of these individualistic values that tell them they need to be independent and not be a burden on others. Yet, insisting on independence or just ending up living alone out of circumstance does not bring the quality of life people might anticipate. More often than not, it brings hardship, loneliness, and loss of well-being.

The new elderhood assumption advocates that we find a support network that works for us in our later years. Those without children—those who most certainly can't rely on the expectation that their children will be there for them when they are old—already have to think like this. Many without children (by choice or not) start planning for when they are old way before they get there. They make long term financial goals and research different types of living situations. Others know how they want to set up their living situation in their elder years, whether living in their own home, a kind of senior community, or even sharing a house with close friend(s). Many without children envision and plan on working to build a support network when they are old, such as relationships with younger family members like nieces and nephews, dear friends, younger people in their lives, and ties to their religious community.

Will not having their kids as their support network negatively impact parents' well-being when they're old? Research tells us it won't. What contributes most to our well-being when we're old? Some studies say having our spouse/partner around and having financial stability. The studies indicate that having your loved one with you and having enough money are keys to well-being.[23] Other studies indicate the importance of having friends in our later years.[24] When it comes to feelings of loneliness, seniors may have their children there, but having friends their own age makes more of a difference.

When asked what advice she would give to people as they plan for their later years, whether they have children or not, researcher Elena Portocolone stresses the importance of making friends with people their own age, as well as making friends with younger people. She suggests making friends with younger social workers or people in similar professions who can be of help. She advises buying a home in a central location that one plans to live in for a long time and getting savvy about all of the services that will be available as part of setting up a support structure—way before these services are needed.

In the larger picture, Elena Portacolone advocates a context that supports taking on the responsibility of developing elderhood support structures. It's the context of "interdependence" or interdependent living. In our later years, we need to have our support network and also ways to stay integrated in the larger social network of our communities for support. She contends that policy is needed to encourage and ensure this kind of support. One way to do this is to strengthen community-based networks of services for seniors. They can be funded so that communities can know who is living alone, who needs assistance, and can help seniors remain actively integrated with different generations. These networks can also be a "platform for help with essential functions" in life, including a minimal level of financial stability to ensure "dignified living."[25]

Support structures close to us and in the larger community reinforce an interdependent lifestyle and living with the attitude that gets at the core of interdependence. It is "built around the idea that everyone needs to be interconnected to succeed and that individuals are fundamentally and inevitably dependent on each other."[26] The Alternative Assumption is about taking charge of that interdependence. It suggests cultivating a support structure way before you need it and building that system of support beyond your children if you have them. Have that structure be comprised of what works best for you, whether it be blood relatives, and/or friends from a variety of ages, and stay connected to the larger community for social engagement and assistance.

Contrary to pronatalist beliefs about the presumed benefit of having children when we are old, the Alternative Assumption gets at the truth that the benefits may not be there. It puts a priority on having a vision for our later years and taking responsibility for making it happen. This vision includes thinking about the financial realities of our later years long before those years arrive, setting savings goals and sticking to them, and making the development of an interdependent elderhood support structure a serious priority. It doesn't rule out help from adult children; it just goes beyond it, making help from them in our later years a welcome addition, not an expected cornerstone of support that may or may not be there.

9

THE TRANSITION HAS ALREADY BEGUN

With our society operating under the old assumptions, when we've found a partner and are living happily ever after, we're invariably asked, "When are you going to start having kids?" These days, more people are answering, "Never." They represent a rising segment of the population that has taken a "red natal pill" and knows about the baby matrix. The "childfree" or "childless by choice" are going against pronatalism's social and cultural norms and are challenging the values and lifestyle of a child-centered society. What do we know about these people? Since the year 2000, more research has been done on them than ever before. The Appendix gives an overview of the different areas of recent research. Here's a snapshot of what we know about this slice of our population.

Highlights of the Latest Research

The U.S. Census Bureau has been tracking "childlessness" (this is the term it uses in its research) numbers for some time now. However, it has not tracked why women do not have children, e.g., whether it's by choice or not. Many Census researchers are of the view, however, that a childless woman who is in the 40-44 age range (the highest age group it studies in this regard) is most likely someone who chose not to have children because medical technology is so advanced and infertility and sterility rates are low.

According to the U.S. Census, from 2000 to 2007, the numbers of women aged 40-44 who did not have children ranged between 18-20 percent.[1] The 2010 U.S. Census report tells us that the numbers have remained about the same. For the year 2008, 18 percent of women aged 40-44 did not have children. In the same age range, U.S. Census figures broken down by race indicate that: 18 percent of white women had no children compared with 18 percent of black women, 13 percent of Asian women, and 19 percent of Hispanic women.[2]

A study released in 2010 by Pew Research Center (PRC) indicates that since 1994, rates of childlessness (the research term used by PRC) for black and Hispanic women increased by more than 30 percent. For whites, rates increased 11 percent.[3] The racial gap has narrowed particularly for blacks and Hispanics. The reasons may relate to education. The more education women of any ethnicity receive, the more they realize that they have choices in life. If women put off having children—whatever their ethnicity—they may end up deciding not to have them. However, Yale researchers Natalie Nitsche and Hannah Brueckner say there can be more to it than putting it off.[4] Black women face a series of challenges when navigating education, career, marriage, and childbearing that often leave them single and with no children, even when they'd prefer marriage and family. Nitsche and Brueckner explain that "marriage chances for highly educated black women have declined over time relative to white women." Contrary to some myths, most educated, professional women who want to marry do marry. But the picture is less bright for high-achieving black women because their "marriage markets" aren't great. It is said that we have a strong tendency to marry someone of our educational level and that this can be hard for black women to do because highly educated black women outnumber highly educated black men. They also say black women are reluctant to marry outside their race. These factors can often make many black women end up childless, but not by choice.

Nadra Kareem Nittle at Change.org thinks there are different *attitudes* about women with no children from different races, however.

She thinks that while the media is not that hard on white women with no children, this is not the case for single, educated black women. The media has also told us that "black women are romantically undesirable because they are too educated and successful for black men and unwilling or unable to pair up with non-blacks." She says that highly educated black women are often seen as "grievous anomalies."[5]

In addition to media-generated perceptions, negative attitudes also stem from cultural considerations. In Hispanic culture, being childfree is seen very negatively. While the numbers of Hispanic women aged 40-44 with no children have risen in recent years, these women are still judged within their culture. So while the numbers are rising, negative perceptions of women with no children remain across and within different races. Some are more general across certain races, such as the perceptions that such women are selfish, immature, and/or hate children. Others within race are sociologically and culturally specific.

Data have also been collected on the educational levels of women who have no children. According to the 2008 U.S. Census, 15 percent of women aged 40-44 who did not graduate from high school did not have children, 15 percent with a high school education did not have children, 22 percent with a bachelor's degree did not have children, and 22 percent with a graduate/professional degree did not have children. Pew Research Center also looked at the educational status of women aged 40-44 with no children. Their 2010 report (using 2006-2008 U.S. Census data) indicated that since "the 1990s, rates of childlessness have risen most sharply for the least educated women. From 1994 to 2008, the likelihood of women with less than a high school diploma not having children rose 66 percent." Rates of women having no children grew less steeply over the same time period among high school graduates and women with some college but not a degree. For women in this age range "with a bachelor's degree, there has been essentially no change in the likelihood of being childless." The report also found a seven percent dip in women aged 40-44 with higher education who did not have children.[6] This figure might reflect an uptick in a trend for more highly educated women starting to have children in their early 40s. It also goes along with the existing trend that women are waiting longer to have children. In this case, it could mean more are waiting even longer into their 40s.

The U.S. Census survey also includes interesting annual family income data on women aged 40-44 with no children: 20 percent had a $20,000-29,999 annual family income range, 20 percent had a $30,000-49,999 annual family income range, 18 percent had a $50,000-74,999 annual family income range, 17 percent had a $75,000-99,999 annual family income range, and 14 percent had a $100,000+ annual family income range.[7] These figures tend to debunk the popular notion that those who don't have children have higher incomes and more disposable cash. Instead, they reflect the reality that people with no children come from all income levels, not just the higher ones.

There is also recent data on marriages with no children. First, attitudes have changed. According to the PRC, in 1990, 65 percent of adults said that children were very important for a successful marriage. In 2007, 41 percent gave this opinion. In its 2010 report using 2008 data, PRC breaks women into the "ever married" category to include those who are married now or who were married at some point in the past, and the "never married." "Among 40-44-year-old ever married women, 13 percent had no children of their own." When the numbers are broken down by ethnicity, for the period ranging from the mid-90s to the 2006-2008, PRC reports increases in ever married whites, blacks, and Hispanics having no children, with the largest increases among married black and Hispanic women.[8]

We also know more about where women with no children live. The 2008 U.S. Census has looked at this and found that 18 percent of women aged 40-44 lived in the northeastern part of the U.S., 17 percent lived in the Midwest, 17 percent lived in the South, and 19 percent lived in the West.[9] This suggests that as of 2008, such women lived in every major region of the U.S., which marks a departure from the decade before (and earlier) when women with no children were more likely to reside on the East and West Coast.

Wherever they live, more women these days are delaying having children. This is so prevalent that the U.S. Census has labeled the phenomenon a "delayer boom."[10] And for many women, the longer they delay having children, the more likely it is they will not end up having children at all. Recent research suggests that people are judging this choice less harshly than in years past. For example, according to a National Opinion Research Center's General Social Survey, in 1988, 39 percent of adults disagreed with the statement that people with no children "lead empty lives." In 2002, 59 percent disagreed with this.[11] Recent research on the Generation X generation shows stronger signs of increased acceptance. With GenXers, we are seeing the highest numbers ever of people with no children. A study released in 2011 by the Center for Worklife Policy reports that "43 percent of Xer women and 32 percent of Xer men are choosing not to have children."[12] It's encouraging to finally see childfree men in large numbers studied along with women. Numbers like this are also a sign that more people are truly realizing that having children is but one path in life.

With each generation, more people are saying no to pronatalism. Thanks to the advances in technology, those foregoing parenthood have never been more seen and heard. The topic is in the media more than ever before. There's a growing host of childfree authors, journalists, and more who are writing and engaging in discussions on the childfree and who are contributing to the acceptance of the idea that our adult lives do not have to revolve around parenthood and children. All of these things have helped the childfree sail out of the tributaries of society and land on the forefront of challenging a parent and child-centric culture.

10

TOWARD A POST-
PRONATAL SOCIETY

Shifting away from pronatalist assumptions is going to take bold, tangible efforts. Until now, I've set forth why it's time for all of us make this shift. In this chapter, I want to speak directly to you about how, together, we can make the alternative Post-Pronatal Assumptions come alive in our personal and professional lives, in our communities, and globally.

In Our Personal Lives

One of the most important ways to make the new assumptions come alive in our personal lives involves our reproductive decisions. As the Offspring Assumption discussion highlights, your personal reproductive decisions carry great power. Take this reality very seriously when making decisions about children and how many to have. If you decide you want the experience of parenthood, lead by example and make the Offspring Assumption real by adopting. If you have to have your own biological child, stop at one. Do you want more children after that? Bring into your family as many non-biological children as you feel you are prepared to raise.

Dealing with Judgments & Pressures

Until more people are living by the Offspring Assumption, those bucking the old assumption will continue to deal with judgments and pressures from others about their decisions related to biological children. If you decide not to have any children, biological or adopted, be ready to face those judgments and pressures head on. To do so, it's important to be well aware of the kinds of pressures you may receive and have a strategy for dealing with them.

One kind of pressure can be called "relational" pressure. It includes comments from friends, family members, or loved ones who want you to have children so that you and they can raise your children together, making your relationship with them even closer. Others also sometimes think they know more about you and what you want than you do. The gist of this type of pressure boils down to comments like, "You will change your mind" or "You may think you don't want a child (or another one) now, but you'll see; that will change." Instead of trying to understand what you feel is right for you, they want to be right *about* you. They sincerely believe that you, too, will eventually do what they believe we all are *supposed* to want to do.

Another type of pressure is guilt-driven. It's intended to make you feel badly about not doing what others want you to do. It can include comments about how you'll be a disappointment to the family or that you'll be responsible for your partner's lack of fulfillment in life. Or if you already have children, such as an only child, others may talk about why this is not good for that child and how s/he needs a brother or sister (which research does not support). Most often, though, gossip operates as a back door to guilt. This is when you learn about others' disappointment and disapproval through someone else. It is designed to make you feel that your decisions negatively affect others you love.

People may go further and put on "nosy to invasive" pressure. This is when those who want you to have children ask you personal questions as to why you don't have kids or don't want to have them. These questions can get invasive when the personal questions go too far, such as asking directly about potential physical or emotional problems or personal decisions like birth control use.

A four-part strategy will relieve the pressure. First, what not to do: lie. In the past, lying has been a more common way of dealing with the pressures. For example, childfree people told those who pressured them to have children that they "couldn't" have children. This explanation led to further concealment and the need to act sad and grief-stricken about it. To move toward living by the Post-Pronatal Assumptions, we have to tell the truth, even when we predict we will hurt or be judged by others. Falsely sending the message that we want a child and that we would have one if we could only continues to reinforce a child-centric belief system that does not support a childfree choice. We need to have the courage to be honest and communicate directly, yet diplomatically.

As far as strategy, if you are not having children, first be very clear in your own mind why you feel this way. Not only do you need to know this for yourself and your partner if you are in a relationship, but you need to know it so that you can articulate it to others. You can use the Post-Pronatal Assumptions you particularly resonate with to help you explain yourself. For example, use the Destiny Assumption to explain that the idea of the biological clock is not true for you and that there is no real evidence that this clock exists at all. Or talk about the Normality Assumption: Explain how there is nothing wrong with not wanting the experience of parenthood. Or use the Fulfillment Assumption, explaining that parenthood brings fulfillment to many people, but it is not "the" way for everyone and not the way for you.

If you are in a relationship, strategy two is to present a united front. This is important because it's easy for others to blame one or the other person in the relationship, but it's harder to do this if *both* people clearly vocalize their position. It also means both parties have done the thinking they need to be ready to verbalize their reasons. In response to any of the judgments or pressures, both parties need to be willing to talk about where they stand.

Strategy three: Nip the pressures in the bud. It's important not to wait to speak up when you feel you are being hit with pressure. The longer you tolerate direct or indirect pressures, your feelings will fester, which will not serve you when you do try to talk to those who are pressuring you. I could tell you many stories in which couples "sat on it" as the interrogation became so intense that they hit a breaking point, resulting in an argument or "blow" that could have been avoided.

And fourth, perhaps the most important step in alleviating pressure is to seek mutual understanding. After honestly and clearly communicating in a heartfelt way where we stand, we need to have the courage to find out why these people are pressuring us. We need to ask them, "Why do *you* want me to have children?" We need to get them to see *what's in it for them*. If it's our parents, and they want grandkids, why specifically do they want a grandchild? Do they have concerns that they will be seen as strange or bad parents if we don't have kids? Are they concerned about how not having kids will affect the relationship with them? Whatever the reason, talk with them until they see how their desires relate to them and their own feelings, not to you. If you can talk openly about why *they* want what they want for you and why *they* judge you for your decision, the pressure will stop 99 percent of the time.

The same steps apply in other situations that don't follow the old pronatal model. You might already have a biological child and get pressure to have another one, or yet another one. The same principles apply: Know your reasons, articulate them, and most importantly, seek mutual understanding. You might take the road of adoption and have no biological children and still get pressure to have "your own." In this case, seeking mutual understanding has to include finding out why it is so important to *them* that you biologically create a child.

Overcoming the pressures that come from the old natal mindset takes self-worth, a brave heart, and effective communication. It can be challenging, especially when you're dealing with loved ones or others who so strongly see the world through a child-centric lens. Yet, as we move away from this lens, pressures will lessen, and so will the need to deal with them.

Exposure & Education

In addition to effectively dealing with pressures from others with the old pronatal mindsets, we can encourage others to look at alternative mindsets. For example, if someone brings up how her biological clock is going off, it's time to talk with her about the Destiny Assumption. When others say they want children, it's time to not shy away from the Right to Reproduce Assumption and even inquire into why they think they *want* children. If others are talking about having children or asking you about this, talk about the Offspring Assumption to educate them on the costs of bringing more biological children into our world. Be willing to broach the idea of why they might consider adoption first over having biological children. Talk about the myths of adoption, and try to make them understand why choosing adoption as their first option, not their last, is truly the selfless choice given the state of the world today.

Any chance we get, we need to be willing to talk about why we need to think differently about what reproductive responsibility means in today's society. Armed with the information in this book, you can point out—when others refer to themes in the old assumptions—why they are either no longer true or incorrect and why it's time to live by a new mindset.

Our Later Years

Along with challenging pronatalism with others, we need to make the Elderhood Assumption come alive and take action to prepare for our later years. This means taking responsibility for our elderhood many years before that time comes. One action involves ensuring affordability of some kind of long term care, whether home care or nursing home care. Research shows that "70% of Americans aged 65 and older will need long term care services at some point in their lives."[1] There is no reason to think that this percentage will decline with upcoming generations or that it won't be something we'll need in our later years. This kind of care has often been expensive, but at the time of this writing, a federal option is expected to become available in the year 2013. The 2010 federal health care law includes the Community Living Assistance Supports and Services plan, or CLASS, a federal long term care insurance option. It is set up to be self-funded through premiums, not taxpayer dollars. With or without children, preparing for long term care needs should be part of one's overall financial plan in addition to retirement accounts. Since research tells us that one of the top contributors to well-being in our later years is financial stability, it's important to make sure we can afford to get old.

Living by the alternative Elderhood Assumption also includes creating a vision for how you want to be able to live your life when you're old. For example: What kind of living environment do you want to be in? What do your financial goals need to be in order to get there over time? What do you envision your support network to look like? What can you do *now* to cultivate that support structure? What long term actions will make your "later years vision" a reality?

In Our Professional Lives

Making the Post-Pronatal Assumptions come alive in the workplace starts with stopping the reinforcement of pronatalism at work. Like other areas of life, there has been widespread parent entitlement and child-centrism in the workplace. We have to stop going along with the mindset that parental commitments come first or that children are somehow the workplace's communal responsibility. How do these mindsets commonly play out? With a "non-parent pick up the slack" culture. A common example includes situations in which parent employees receive flextime so that they can tend to child-related activities. It's expected that the non-parents pick up their slack, and the non-parents do it.

Why has the "pick up the slack" culture been so pervasive in many workplaces? Because of pronatalist perceptions that parental commitments are more valuable or more important than non-parental commitments. In a 2011 study released by the Center for Work Life Policy, 60 percent of female non-parents and 36 percent of male non-parents felt that their colleagues with children perceived non-parent personal commitments as less important than those of colleagues with children.[2] According to Sylvia Ann Hewlett, the founding president of the Center for Work Life Policy, "non-parents feel that all the best benefits are going to one demographic: those who are married with small kids."[3]

Non-parents' feelings are justified. There are many kinds of benefits and policies that support working parents, including paid parental leave, flextime options, and telecommuting options. Policies that support non-parental personal commitments are rare or nonexistent. This lack of equitable time-off policies is not a new phenomenon; it has been the case for some time. In *Baby Boon: How Family-Friendly America Cheats the Childless*, author Elinor Burkett discusses this longstanding inequitable workplace culture. She speaks about the unwritten, yet widely adhered to, "10 Commandments of workplace etiquette in family-friendly America," which include the sort of attitudes non-parents should abide by and that parents expect to. These include: "Thou shalt volunteer to work late so that mothers can leave at 2:00 p.m. to watch their sons play soccer" and "Thou shalt never ask for a long leave to write a book, travel, or fulfill thy heart's desire because no desire other than children could possibly be worth thy company's inconvenience."[4]

Rejecting this "parent-child come first" orientation as it plays out in the workplace will bring more equal treatment for all employees and will reflect a mindset that parents and their children are no more important than others who do not have children. Non-parents have felt this way for many years, but these days, more non-parents are beginning to speak up and ask for personal time-off policies that reflect equal treatment of employees with and without children. Instead of parents only getting personal leave, non-parents want all employees, regardless of parental status, to get this kind of leave. They also want non-parents and parents alike to receive the same flextime options or opportunities to telecommute.

If inequitable leave and flextime policies exist in your workplace, the bold action is to ask for the development or refinement of inequitable policies that stem from whether the employee has children or not (or is pregnant and is about to become a parent). Be willing to ask for policies that don't treat parents preferentially just because they made the choice to become parents. At first, some coworkers who are parents may balk at this and not understand why these kinds of policies are necessary. Be willing to talk with them and make the point that, like discrimination based on race, gender, or sexual preference, these kinds of policies seek equal treatment for all employees, no matter who they are or the lifestyle they choose.

In Our Communities

To move toward a Post-Pronatal Society, the "parent-child come first" default orientation also needs to change in our communities. Take our behavior in public places. Pronatalism has taught us that we need to put children first in public places. For example, on public transportation, such as buses, subways, and the like, it has become common etiquette to give up your seat for a child and accommodate all the accoutrements that go with kids today, such as large strollers. On elevators, we are supposed to let kids, parents, and their accoutrement on first. Instead of this default, we need to begin to act more from a "person-oriented" mindset. In public, it means asking what *person*, no matter what age, looks like they need to go first or take the seat, such as the elderly, disabled, or even just a person with a lot of packages. A "person-first" orientation certainly can include parents and children; it's just that we would no longer always defer to the needs of children and their parents first.

Pronatalism has also taught us to tolerate children's disruptive behavior or ineffectual parents in public places, and we're supposed to do this as much as possible before we attempt to deal with the situation. Even if we do reach a point of intolerance, it's still taboo to say something about the noise or disruption. When we change the context from "kids and parents first" to "people first," situations like these become more about a baseline of respect for *all* of those involved. No longer are parents and children entitled to disrespect others' space or disrupt others in public. Respect for everyone, regardless of age or reproductive role, is valued. To reinforce a mindset of equal respect for all, when we're subjected to a disruptive child or ineffective parental behavior, we need to be willing to respectfully speak out (and not wait until it is intolerable), asking for that respect. We will still run up against resistance from those who still come from a pronatalist place, but the more we respectfully challenge it, the more the old assumptions surrounding parent-child entitlement in public will weaken.

In some respects, we already see evidence of a transition from kids and parents first to a people-first orientation in some public spheres. For example, Alamo Drafthouse Theaters in Texas and Virginia have policies that respect the movie-going experience for everyone. They have no tolerance for disruption. If there is an adult or group of adults being obnoxious, loud, lewd, or the like, you let the server know, and the disturber(s) will be asked to stop and/or will be immediately escorted from the theater. There is also the rule of no texting during the show; if a person keeps texting, they will be asked to leave. The theaters also make it a general rule not to admit children under six years of age. In the words of CEO Tim League, "If the movie is a non-crossover kids' movie, we sometimes flex this age down to three and up, and we also have select 'Baby Day' screenings each week for (families with) infants and small children. If you want to take your four-year-old to see 'The Hangover 2' at 10 p.m., however, you'll have to go somewhere else." The theaters also do not allow unaccompanied minors. What have been the results of these kinds of policies? Loyal patrons.

In other public arenas, policies that support respect for all may not have changed, but surveys indicate that people would like them to change. Take air travel. When it comes to children, pronatalism leads us to believe that we're supposed to tolerate disruption on planes. However, according to a recent survey by Skyscanner.net, 59 percent of travelers, parents and non-parents, say they would prefer something other than the mindset that we just accept disruptive children in this situation. They said they liked the idea of a "family-only" section on flights.[5] Another recent survey of 1,000 passengers, parents and non-parents, found that half would pay higher ticket prices to avoid kids in the main cabin.[6] Now, parents and children are not always the source of disruption or lack of respect; there are many ways this happens on planes as a result of people of all ages. However, it has been more acceptable to challenge disrespecting adults than parents and their disruptive children on an aircraft, and this is what needs to change.

One of the most powerful ways to create change toward more of a "people-first" orientation is through purchasing power. Give your business to companies that you see are going beyond the attitude, "we're all supposed to cater first to kids." Whether dining out, at stores, public events, traveling, or in any other public place, support the attitude that everyone, no matter what age, is just as important as another, and purchase from those whose business practices reflect the same.

The Larger Society

The biggest ways you can help make the Post-Pronatal Assumptions come alive on a larger level start with the Right to Reproduce and Offspring Assumptions. Here are some ways to take needed action. Get involved in initiatives for parenthood education in your local school districts, including pushing for curriculum that presents parenthood as an option, not a given in life. Seek out and support nongovernmental organizations (NGOs) that are involved in parenthood education, particularly ones that promote parenthood as a choice, such as family planning and reproductive rights groups or organizations concerned with population issues. One NGO that focused on the mission of parenthood as a choice was the National Alliance for Optional Parenthood (NAOP). It existed for ten years from 1972 to 1982. Its purpose was to "educate the public on non-parenthood as a valid lifestyle option, support those who choose not to have children, promote awareness of the overpopulation problem."[7] It was funded by some of the most respected foundations, including Rockefeller Brothers and the William & Flora Hewlett Foundation. In the Hewlett Foundation's 1981 annual report, it described NAOP as an organization that "encourages young people to make thoughtful and responsible decisions about parenting by trying to reduce the impact of societal pressures that equates success or growing up with parenthood." It did some great work, including print and broadcast media campaigns to "stimulate thought and discussion concerning alternatives to parenthood, and to sensitize the public and media on the forces that encourage and unrealistically romanticize parenthood."[8] It had a volunteer network in 30 states and a national referral network of people who counseled or presented workshops on decision-making about parenthood.

As the new assumptions begin to take hold, the odds are you will see a resurgence of this type of organization and similar campaigns within existing non-profit organizations. When you see these kinds of efforts, get involved and support them! Better yet, start your own. The NAOP started with two dedicated women (one a mother and one not) and grew into an organization that did much to promote a needed social change. It's time to bring their mission back to life.

Send government the message that it's time to treat parenthood as a privilege. Using the information in this book, write your lawmakers and Congresspersons regarding the need for national parent qualification efforts, such as the type of required certification program outlined in this book. Speak out about why child tax credit policies need to be changed from creating incentives that encourage the birth of children to providing incentives for adoption and the reduction in biological births. Support organizations that are working toward these types of goals at all governmental levels.

On a global scale, we can make the Offspring Assumption come alive by getting involved in global reproductive health and family planning efforts. They comprise a critical strategy for reducing births around the world in order to try and achieve a sustainable population. Many population experts, such as those at the organization Population Matters, the working name of the Optimum Population Trust, believe that "family planning is the most effective way to reduce the likelihood of catastrophic global warming."[9] Better global access to birth control will result in better family planning and fewer births. Some recent numbers paint the picture showing why these efforts need to be supported. In less developed nations, the total fertility rate is 4.5 children per woman. In sub-Saharan Africa, only 22 percent of women use contraception. Globally, 215 million women who want to avoid pregnancy are not using an effective method of contraception, and the demand for contraception is expected to increase by 40 percent by 2050. What kind of family planning funding is needed? About $6.7 billion a year. That sounds like a lot until you consider that the U.S. military budget is almost $2 billion *per day.*[10]

It's clear that over four children per woman is not the road to stabilizing our population. To support the future of our world and the people already on it, we need to promote the reduction of births globally, along with efforts to make national and inter-country adoption processes as effective as possible. In any way we can, we need to educate others about why the fewer biological births a woman has, the better it will be for all. By becoming involved in these kinds of larger scale efforts, you will be part of the movement working toward a more survivable world.

Adopting the Post-Pronatal Assumptions Will:

- Free us from social controls that ultimately only serve the survival of societal power structures

- Create fuller expression of our human identity

- Allow us to seek meaning in our lives as we define it

- Create a society with the highest levels of reproductive responsibility

- Free us from a longstanding prejudicial cultural context that prevents full reproductive freedom

- Promote self-directed responsibility in our later years

- Enhance the possibility of achieving population stabilization with finite resources

Like those who "freed their minds" in the movie *The Matrix*, it's time to free ourselves from a pronatalist mindset. We've been chipping away at pronatalism for a while now, with the continued rise of those who are bucking the parent-child-centric way of life. But as the new assumptions make clear, it's time for bolder moves away from pronatalist beliefs because that is all they are; they don't represent reality and don't serve us in the state of the world as it is today. It's time to move to a Post-Pronatal era in order to progress as a society and ensure its survival in the future.

The 7 Post-Pronatal Assumptions

The Destiny Assumption

Our biological capacities allow us to make parenthood a choice.

The Normality Assumption

It is just as normal to not want children as it is to want them.

The Marriage Assumption

People marry as a way to bring them happiness and fulfillment in life.

The Right to Reproduce Assumption

Parenthood is a privileged right.

The Offspring Assumption

Decisions on having children put one's obligation to the planet first.

The Fulfillment Assumption

Parenthood is one path to purpose and fulfillment in life.

The Elderhood Assumption

Finding my elderhood support structure is my responsibility.

APPENDIX

Research Highlights on the Childfree From the Year 2000

In 2000, U.S. Census data indicated that 19 percent of women, almost one in five, aged 40-44 had no children.[1] Demographics on women with no children were also out on several fronts. Starting with race, about 20 percent of white women aged 40-44 had no children. About 18 percent of black women aged 40-44 did not have children, and 21 percent of Asian/Pacific Islander women in the same age range did not have children. The number of Hispanics in this group was lower at about 11 percent.[2] Data also told us that women aged 40-44 with no children tended to have higher levels of education, middle to upper middle class incomes, and worked in managerial, technical, sales, and administration occupations. Overall, employed women showed the highest increases in childlessness, and in the United States, they tended to live in the West and Northeast.[3]

There were also theories that those who had no children by choice were more likely to be the oldest child or only child and that they came from troubled family backgrounds, but those theories weren't supported by the research. According to Stuart Basten at St. John's College, Oxford and Vienna Institute of Demography, studies indicated that birth order, size of family, and perceived parental happiness were not related to childlessness.[4] Those with no children by choice were no more likely to come from troubled backgrounds than people who grew up to become parents. But there was widespread agreement that the childfree were less apt to adopt traditional and conventional gender roles and were less likely to consider themselves religious.

Why did people say no to children? A minority knew early in life that they just did not have the desire to be a mother or father and were called "early articulators." For most, though, the decision happened over time and came to a head when in a relationship. The most common reasons people gave for not wanting children included concerns about how having a child would affect the couple's relationship and what it would mean for their life together financially. Many couples had concerns about the lifestyle parenthood would create and how child rearing would impact their ability to reach other goals in life. Others looked at a bigger picture and decided they did not want to bring another human being onto an already crowded planet.

However, behind situational, contextual, or more logical reasons was a simple lack of emotional desire to be a parent. It was a decision that ultimately came from the heart. If the desire was strong enough, odds were that people would mentally reconfigure their concerns and be more apt to believe kids would enhance, not hurt, the relationship. They might more easily believe they could make it work financially, that they would still be able to reach important goals, albeit later, or even that they could raise a child who would contribute to solving some of the world's environmental problems.[5]

Back then, were marriages happier without children? At that time, a good number of studies suggested that marriages with no children by choice were the happiest of all. Other studies found that marital satisfaction declined when children entered the equation, but over the long term, those declines weren't markedly different from what couples who never had children experienced. Still other findings suggested that the cycles of satisfaction for parents and non-parents were just different. With parents, it was more of a u-shaped curve, starting high, dipping when the children came on the scene, then climbing again when they were grown and gone. With childfree couples on the other hand, it tended to improve slowly and steadily over time.

In 2000, *Families of Two* took us into the lives of the happily married childfree. The book is based on interviews with over 100 childfree couples. For the first time in a book on the childfree, we heard from the couples themselves up close and personal and saw them in photos. And unlike many other books at the time, we heard directly from childfree men. *Families of Two's* research both concurred with and differed from the prevailing research. For example, most of the childfree couples interviewed were found in the West and Northeast, and most were college educated. However, most did not come from higher socioeconomic classes, but from various socioeconomic backgrounds. They tended to be middle class, and they worked in a variety of occupations.

At the time, the common picture of the childfree woman was someone who chose her career over motherhood. While this was the case for some, many childfree women interviewed for *Families of Two* did not say their career was the reason they decided not to have children. While most childfree men and women said they were not particularly religious, a good number of them said their religious life was very important to them. Some also indicated that they had less than traditional gender roles in their relationships.

At the time, there were many myths about the childfree. They were very often perceived as selfish and self-absorbed people. They were also commonly seen as immature, unwilling to take on the responsibilities of adulthood, or not wanting to "grow up." Despite the fact that children played a role in many of their personal and professional lives, they were also very commonly perceived as strongly disliking children.

In the years to follow, we saw a surge of research that looked at these things and more.

Highlights of Recent Research

In the decade following the year 2000, more research was conducted on those with no children than ever before. Studies covered a variety of areas, but many of them occurred in these areas: not having children in one's later years, motives for making the childfree decision, perceptions/attitudes of the childfree, gender identity issues, marriage, and international studies.

Having No Children in Later Years

A good deal of recent research into the childfree choice has explored the elder years and been conducted cross-nationally. Pearl Dykstra of the Hague Utrecht University in the Netherlands has been a key contributor to this area of study. In her *Journal of Family Issues* article, "Roads Less Taken: Developing a Nuanced View of Older Adults Without Children," Dykstra argues that it's important to study childless older adults, to not "overlook diversity in life experience," and to not "assume deficiencies" of those in the minority.[6]

Some studies looked at how people ended up without children in their later years. A minority of women knew earlier in life that they did not want children, and they entered into their retirement years having never had them. However, for most men and women, reaching the decision to be childfree was a gradual process stemming from a series of choices made throughout the course of their lives. Gunhild Hagestad at the Norwegian Social Research Institute and Vaughn Call of Brigham Young University looked at how "delayed transitions" can play an important role in ending up without children in old age.[7] An example of a delayed transition is marrying later; delaying marriage can increase the chances a couple would not have kids. Another delayed transition could have to do with a career path; depending on where a career took a person, it could influence a delay in having children and eventually lead to not having them at all.

Much of the aging research in recent history has asked in one way or another, "Are the childless less emotionally healthy in their later years than people who had children?" Research findings suggest the answer is no. A large study conducted by the University of South Florida looked at the lives of over 800 retirees and found no differences between adults without children and adults who were parents in terms of self-esteem, psychological well-being, and life satisfaction.[8] Australian and Israeli researchers Julie Cwikel, Helen Gramotnev, and Christina Lee found similar results in their studies of women who had never married and had no children. They found no differences in emotional (or physical) health and that single, childfree women are just as likely as parents to have fulfilling later years. In fact, the researchers indicate that their "life experiences and opportunities prepare them for successful and productive old age."[9]

Pearl Dykstra found the better predictor of life satisfaction in later years is marital history, not parental history.[10] Research conducted at the Population Research Institute and Department of Sociology at Pennsylvania State University by Z. Zhang and M.D. Hayward also indicated that there is no support for the hypothesis that a life without parenthood means higher levels of depression for divorced, widowed, and never married older persons.[11] Contrary to some popular thinking, the sole factor of not having children did not predict loneliness or depression. Instead, when coupled with the absence of children, gender and marital status proved to be the better predictors of emotional well-being. In this study, women fared better than the men; divorced men with no children, widowed men with no children and men who had never married and had no children had higher rates of loneliness compared to women with the same background. Divorced and widowed men with no children also had higher levels of depression than divorced and widowed women with no children.

Regina Bures, Tanja Koropeckyj-Cox and Michael Loree at the University of Florida studied depressive symptoms in middle-aged and older adults. They found that adults with no children had the lowest predicted levels of depression across all marital status groups. Widowed men had higher levels of depression than other men. Never married biological mothers and formerly married women who had outlived their children averaged higher levels of depression.[12]

Other researchers have identified another predictor of depressive symptoms in later life: net worth. According to a longitudinal health and retirement study at the University of Michigan, one's net worth is an independent predictor of depressive symptoms. At the University of Washington, Robert Plotnick's research supports this finding. He studied older married and unmarried men and women and found that it is not children, but wealth, that contributes most to one's well-being.[13]

Studies also tell us that well-being is affected when women are voluntarily childfree versus involuntarily childless. Take, for example, a study done by researchers Sherryl Jeffries and Candace Konnert. They looked at well-being and regret among the middle-aged and older childfree, the "involuntarily" childless, and mothers. They found that childfree women displayed higher levels of well-being than women who wanted children but did not have them.[14] They also found that they had less child-related regret than involuntarily childless women.

Other studies looked at whether the childfree are more isolated and lonely in old age than parents. Surveys show this is not the case. According to researcher Dr. Melinda Forthofer, "the social networks of the childless can be just as rich, just as full, as parents." She conducted a study of over 850 retirees and found little differences in psychosocial well-being between those with and without children. In fact, those with no children tended to have larger social networks and lead more active social lives than parents.[15]

Other studies that focus on the social lives of the older childfree have found that those with children and without children tend to be equally active socially. Researchers G. Clare Wenger, Pearl Dykstra, Tuula Melkas, and Kees C.P.M. Knipscheer looked at people with no children across countries (United States, U.K., Australia, Finland, Germany, Israel, Netherlands, and Spain) and learned that those with no children were just as likely to be active in their communities and volunteer organizations as older persons who are parents. In some countries, marriage, rather than parenthood, made the difference in terms of strength of support networks.[16] A study by Dykstra found that those with no children can have smaller social networks, but there still weren't any differences in sociability between the two groups.[17]

Whether the social networks are smaller, the same, or larger than parents' social networks, research tells us that overall, the childfree don't suffer later in life from a lack of well-being more than parents. Some studies have gone further and asked the question, "Do those without children have higher mortality risks than parents?" These kinds of studies have had mixed results. Researcher Emily Grundy from the Center for Population Studies at the London School of Hygiene and Tropical Medicine conducted a few studies that looked at mortality and fertility history. One study looked at women in the U.K., Norway, and the United States. Grundy found that women with no children had higher risks of earlier death and poor health in later life, as did mothers of five or more children, teenage mothers, and mothers who had children with less than an 18-month gap between births.[18] Grundy says that reasons behind these findings are complicated and that "biosocial pathways" that link reproduction and health need more study. Overall, though, the studies show that it isn't just a phenomenon due to the absence of children. Might one biosocial pathway have to do with the desire to have children? It would be interesting to more deeply examine whether women who had no children *not* by choice are more likely to have higher risks of death and poor health in life than those who consciously chose not to have them.

Researchers have looked at men's mortality as well. Studies have shown that older men with no children who are living alone have a higher risk of dying sooner than fathers living with one of their children. However, fathers living alone also have a higher risk of dying sooner than fathers living with a child.[19] Here, too, not having children doesn't seem to be the determining factor, but possibly one reason in a larger web of social and health factors.

Why People Decide Not to Have Children

In recent years, research on why people make the decision to be childfree has reinforced and built on research before it. Theories on what motivates people not to have children have also expanded. For example, researcher Rosemary Gillespie developed a framework for looking at what motivates people to be childfree, and it has two parts. The first involves a set of factors that point to an attraction, or "pull" to not have children. Wanting the experience of freedom in life "pulls" people toward wanting to be childfree, as does wanting a better relationship with one's partner and believing they will be happier without offspring. The second set has to do with a "push away" from motherhood.[20] A concern about losing one's identity to the identity of "mother" can "push" a woman away from motherhood. So can just a lack of interest in activities typically associated with motherhood.

Studies by sociologist Kristin Park reinforced previous research. She conducted in-depth interviews and focus group research with women and found that a lack of maternal instinct and interest in children motivated women to not want children. Other women saw children as conflicting with their career identities and leisure pursuits.[21] These findings dovetailed with the sentiments of childfree women who reported concerns about how having children would change their work lives and other areas of their lives that were important to them. In the end, the level of desire they had to have kids did not outweigh these kinds of concerns.

Why did men decide not to have children? Recent research reinforced prior trend studies suggesting that they opted out of fatherhood because of the financial sacrifices they saw in raising children. Often, men witnessed firsthand the sacrifices their fathers or other male family members endured to provide for their children. One study involved almost 800 men and indicated that "financial restraints" were among the most frequently cited reasons to say no to parenthood.[22]

Other studies have looked at life circumstances and "pathways" that lead people to choose not to have children. Researchers Renske Keizer, Pearl Dykstra, and Miranda Jansen looked at the lives of about 2,800 women and 2,200 men aged 40 to 79 and examined to what extent educational and employment histories influenced them not to have children. They found different pathways for men and women.[23] For women, the more education they had increased the likelihood of them remaining without children. Similar to Park's research, studies indicate that women who put a high priority on their careers opt out of motherhood because of concerns about how it will impact career goals. A stable career increases the likelihood a woman will not have children, but that's not the case for men. With men, a stable career increases the likelihood they will have children.

Recent research has looked more at how pathways of education and career can lead to postponing parenthood and, ultimately, deciding not to have children at all. The research of Ariene Kemkes Grottenthaler tells a familiar story. She looked at women "postponers," as they have been called. She examined the motivations of academicians who had a lot invested in their careers, and found that some outwardly rejected motherhood. Others kept putting off the decision to a point in life where they felt it was too late, and while they ultimately chose not to have them, it felt like a forced choice.[24] Research by Dylan Kneale and Heather Joshi goes a bit further and explores the rise in "perpetual" postponers. It suggests that postponing parenthood is not just something that relates to women with career aspirations and goals. They found that the process of delaying parenthood among those born in 1970 was more striking for highly qualified men than highly qualified women. What Kneale and Joshi theorized matches what many couples say—that deciding to continue to delay children is often very much a joint decision.[25]

Attitudes and Perceptions of the Childfree

In recent years, we have continued to see research on the negative attitudes and perceptions about the childfree. A number of studies have gone further and explored how the childfree manage how others see them. These studies have been referred to as "stigma management" studies. Researcher Kristin Park conducted a stigma management study that focused on how childfree men and women manage their "stigmatized identity" as childfree people and preserve a positive sense of self. Like other stigma management studies, Park found that the childfree do a host of things to manage the stigmas they face, including being less social than they might otherwise be. By socializing less, they will not have to associate with those they think will judge them negatively for not wanting to be parents. Another way they manage the stigma is to substitute another "identity" for the childfree identity and make that identity paramount, such as the identity of an artist, entrepreneur, etc.

Some also use another kind of stigma management strategy that is more defensive in nature. Parks calls this one "condemning the condemnors." In other words, they manage the stigma by judging those who are judging them. We see examples of this on the Internet, on blogs, and on discussion boards where childfree people share their negative attitudes and perceptions about those with children.

Others manage the stigma indirectly by buying into the norms. One common way they do this is by being less than truthful about their childfree status. They claim that they're childless because they can't have children, even though they can. The childfree think they will be judged less harshly if others think they "can't" have children than if they knew they could have them but are electing not to do so. They would rather others felt sorry for them than criticize them for not being parents.

Kristin Park also speaks to more "proactive" ways to manage the stigmas. One way involves being more direct with others about your right to do what makes you happy and fulfilled in life. Another is not hiding childfree status and being more willing to talk openly about how it's a legitimate and socially valuable lifestyle choice.[26]

In addition to stigma management studies, there has been interesting research examining attitudes and perceptions of the childfree based on how they are portrayed in educational environments. Researchers Laurie Chancey and Susan Dumais at Louisiana State University did a content analysis on college textbooks and were the first to look at how sociology textbooks portray the "voluntary childless" (this is the term most often used in the textbooks in this study). They performed content analyses of twenty marriage and family textbooks that were published and widely used in undergraduate sociology courses between 1950 and 2000.[27]

When they studied books from the 50s, not so surprisingly, they found that the attitude toward those who did not have children by choice was not positive; they were seen as "faint at heart" and "not up to the challenge of parenting." In the 60s, the words in the textbooks reflected more tolerance, and mostly portrayed this status in the context of marriage. The studies outlined in these textbooks mirror what more research has shown—that the presence or absence of children, or the number of children, does not predict marital happiness. When the *Population Bomb* by Paul Ehrlich and David Brower hit the shelves, this choice was discussed in more of an environmental context. In the 1970s, in the textbook, *Men, Women, and Change: A Sociology of Marriage and Family*, authors Scanzoni and Scanzoni first used the term "childfree" to describe study samples. In it the choice was explained in a positive way, and more from a women's rights and environmental movement stance:

> "[W]ith growing concern about population pressures, food and energy shortages, crowding, and all the related problems of too many people on too small a planet, the accusation of selfishness has been aimed toward a different target. Couples who want the rewards of children in great abundance are the ones who are now likely to be labeled self-indulgent and unconcerned about the good of humanity. Couples who forgo the experience of parenthood may be considered by others to be altruistic."[28]

In the 80s, there was a spike in scholarly research in textbooks on this subject. It was the time when textbooks introduced the ideas of "early articulators" and "postponers." Overall, the language used in textbooks had a "tolerant" and "balanced" flavor. For example, the narrative would include statements like, "Despite many people's beliefs, couples who choose to remain childless are usually neither frustrated nor unhappy," and "That careers are prioritized and childcare is a burden sounds like a masculine motivation, but it isn't necessarily so."

Voluntary childlessness showed up less in textbooks in the 90s, but when it did, it tended to continue what the 80s started in terms of dispelling myths associated with not having children by choice. Textbooks supported the idea that it was brave to go against the norm with this decision. Chancey and Dumais contrast perceptions portrayed in textbooks from the 1950s, when it was considered brave to take on the challenge of raising children. Interestingly, by the 90s, "brave" meant something totally different in this regard; the braver choice was not to have them.[29]

Recent studies have also looked at overall societal acceptance of having no children by choice. Researchers Tanya Koropeckyj-Cox and Gretchen Pendell looked at potential differences between men and women on this score, and found that women were more likely to have a more accepting attitude than men. The widest gap between men and women occurred between highly educated men and women in their childbearing years. Highly educated women of childbearing age, whether "temporarily or intentionally childless" (again, these are terms used in the research), had more positive attitudes about this choice than men.[30] Researchers theorized that highly educated men may have had less acceptance because they one day wanted to have children themselves.

Female Gender Identity

In recent years, we've seen some research on motherhood and female gender identity, but there has been little real advancement in this area since psychologist and author Mardy Ireland's pioneering thinking in the 1990s with *Reconceiving Women*. Ireland presents three pathways to female adult identity without motherhood. There is the "Traditional Childless" woman, the "Transitional, Childfree and Childless" woman, and the "Transformative Childfree" woman. The Traditional Childless woman identifies with the stereotypical female gender role which associates femininity with motherhood. She has said "yes" to motherhood, but her body has said "no." With Transitional Childfree and Childless women, "whether it is due to their own ambivalence (about motherhood), poor timing of relationships, or other formidable circumstances," such as wanting to achieve certain career goals before having children, they reach the end of their childbearing years without children. The Transformative Childfree woman chooses not to pursue motherhood, and does not need to have a child to develop her adult feminine identity. These women "are giving birth to additional forms for female identity" because their female experience does not include maternity.[31]

For some time, researchers and academics have been trying to figure out how to define female identity when it does not include motherhood. For example, in *Feminist Review*, Myra Hird writes of how childless women challenge psychoanalytic theories that espouse "normal" gender identification, and development occurs only when a woman has a child.[32] Despite psychoanalytic theory, many women clearly reach normal adult development without this experience. Rosemary Gillespie at the University of Portsmouth agrees. She says that women who choose not to have children are creating the emergence of a new "radical feminine identity."[33]

Others have put forth theories on a new kind of feminine identity without motherhood. Professor Christine Brooks of the Institute of Transpersonal Psychology has posited that Peter Taubman's "model of callings" process of identity formation can apply to "early articulator" women, or women who decide early in life they do not want children. The "model of callings" is one in which "repeated acts of responding to that which hails a person" constitutes the process by which one's identity is formed.[34] In essence, Brooks asks whether a woman's identity is formed out of what she feels called to do and examines how heeding that call can form the process by which she finds her identity, even when it does not involve motherhood. As part of their "call," in her interviews, Brooks found that early articulator women felt they were destined to contribute to society in some way other than motherhood. Psychologist James Hillman might very well agree with this thinking on "calling," as he has considered "the call" to be one's destiny; it is not just vocation, but the "very elements of who a person becomes."[35]

The way Rosemary Balsam of the Western New England Institute of Psychoanalysis looks at women's gender identity in general can also relate to the gender identity of women without children. She makes the case that despite advances in female development theory since the 1970s, there remains a tendency to "stereotype and polarize" gender identity. She thinks of mature female gender identity development as an "interweaving pattern" of body image and identifications. A combination of "paternal" identification and "maternal" female body image and identification ultimately create a woman's identity.[36] This idea can reinforce Ireland's thinking about the Transformative Childfree woman. Ireland talks about how Transformative Childfree women can possess characteristics commonly associated with a traditional male sex role, such as autonomy, assertiveness, and leadership capacity, and how we can see this kind of woman's mature identity as a unique combination of masculine and feminine energy.

Ireland takes things further, asking whether the masculine energy we see in a Transformative Childfree woman is really masculine at all. Why can't the "masculine" aspects truly reflect a reclaiming of unrecognized aspects of feminine energy? Balsam might very well agree. This view takes less of a stereotypical view of gender identity and begins to allow masculine and feminine to fuse to create additional forms of female identity. It also allows the concept of identity to go beyond gender and takes the discussion to elements that make up a *personal* identity. This type of thinking has opened up the possibility of focusing more on *human* development, not just gender development, when it comes to understanding women without children in our society.

Happiness in Marriage & Life

Journalist Lorraine Ali has described recent research on childfree marriage as "redeeming" for the childfree.[37] Some of the largest and most extensive studies in recent years show that childfree marriages are indeed happier. For example, in 2003, researchers W. Keith Campbell and Jean Twenge analyzed almost 100 studies from the 1970s looking at marital satisfaction when couples had children. They found that couples' overall marital satisfaction went down if they had kids, and even more interesting, parents' marital satisfaction has declined with every successive generation.[38] Robin Simon, a sociology professor at Florida State University, saw similar results. In 2005, he looked at data collected from 13,000 Americans by the National Survey of Families and Households, and found that "no group of parents—married, single, step or even empty nest—reported significantly greater emotional well-being than people who never had children."[39] Author Arthur Brooks speaks of similar study results in his book, *Gross National Happiness*, that came out in 2008. He reports that non-parents are happier than parents by about seven percentage points.[40]

Daniel Gilbert, a Harvard professor of psychology, speaks to marital happiness in his book, *Stumbling on Happiness*. Like in past research, he looked at several studies and concludes that marital satisfaction decreases dramatically after the birth of the first child. However, unlike past research that indicated that satisfaction increased over time after the birth of a child, Gilbert found that marital satisfaction increases only when the last child has left home.[41] Other studies indicate that satisfaction declines in cycles, decreasing, for example, when the baby is born, increasing between the kids' ages of six and twelve, and diving again when the kids reach their teens.

In 2006, the National Marriage Project (NMP) gives us their explanation on why childfree marriages can be happier in their report, "The State of Our Unions." Like the research on marriage that came out in 2005 by Pew Research Center, NMP reported that most Americans today say they marry because they believe it will give them greater fulfillment in life. They want an "enduring relationship of love, friendship and emotional intimacy." And cultivating the relationship takes time, attention, and commitment. As NMP says, "Like new babies, contemporary marriages have to be nurtured and coddled in order to thrive. The problem is that once a real baby comes along, the time, effort, and energy that goes into nurturing the relationship goes into nurturing the infant. As a result, marriages can become less happy and satisfying during the child-rearing years."[42]

How else would parenthood affect one's happiness? In her extensive 2010 *New York Times Magazine* article, journalist Jennifer Senior talks about how children are long past being needed (e.g., in pre-urbanization times) to now being a huge expense and more like "projects to be perfected."[43] Not only is parenthood a lot of work, but it creates a lot of unnecessary stress for parents. To psychologist Gail Saltz, "perfect parenting" has become a "competitive sport."[44] Alex Barzvi, a professor of child and adolescent psychiatry at New York University School of Medicine, echoes this belief and contends that modern parents spend lots of energy comparing themselves to other parents and their kids with others' kids, often concluding they're doing the wrong thing. Getting caught up in self-judgment doesn't foster feelings of happiness.

However, research has also looked at happy parents. Happier parents live in countries that have strong social systems that include paid maternity and paternity leave, subsidized childcare, and free education and healthcare. Countries with these kinds of services make parenting easier, and easier parenting makes for happier parents. Even so, better social systems aren't the key to happy parents. As Senior puts it, "*purpose* is happiness."[45] She makes the point that the process of parenting may not make many parents happy these days, but the overall sense of meaning and reward that comes from parenting ultimately defines happiness in the big picture of their lives. As the childfree know, married or not, parenthood is not the *only* way to find purpose and happiness in life.

International Trends

A lot of international research has been done in recent years on people with no children. Much of it has looked at the rising numbers in various countries. For example, in 2003, a large survey funded by the Economic and Social Research Council (ESRC) in the U.K. used the largest samples of data on those with no children ever studied at the time and looked at data from the 1990s across 25 European countries. In part, the survey asked whether infertility accounted for rises in childlessness and concluded it did not.[46] According to the U.N.-sponsored World Fertility Survey, as far back as the mid 1980s, only two to three percent of childfree women between the ages of 25 and 50 were childless due to infertility. The survey concluded that "primary infertility cannot account for the rise in childlessness."[47] U.S. Census researchers have agreed with this conclusion.[48]

The ESRC survey also found that in all countries it looked at, more men than women did not want children. Compared to men, women were more likely to be "keen" on having children and also "seen to be the most likely to regret it." With the exception of Austria, across countries, generally speaking, women felt more ambivalent about not having children. Many women could be classified as what has been termed "perpetual postponers." They continued to delay their decision to have children because of ongoing situational factors, such as their work lives. For example, half of women in higher professional and managerial positions in England did not have children, and half of them reported not having them by choice.

Researcher Donald Rowland at Australian National University also looked at historical trends in childlessness from large surveys, censuses, and national registers across Australia, Europe, America, and Japan. He found the trends to be remarkably similar across these countries. Not having children is trending upward in all of these countries.[49] Starting with Germany, the childless numbers have been rising since the 1990s. In 2002, of women born in 1960 (age 42 at the time), 27 percent had not had children. In a 2008 study by researcher Toshihiko Hara, of those born in West Germany in 1967 (age 41 at the time), 28 percent did not have children.[50] In 2005, according to Luke Harding in *The Guardian*, 30 percent of all women in Germany had no children—the highest proportion in the world.[49] Just looking at women in their 40s, however, recent figures from the Organisation for Economic Co-operation and Development revealed that 20 percent of German women born in 1965 did not have children.[52]

Researchers Yve Stobel-Richter, Manfred Beutel, Carolyn Fink, and Elmar Brahler examined why some Germans choose not to have children.[53] They found people had big concerns about the costs of raising children. Age was also a factor. By the time many women finish college and get a job, they are already in their 30s, which can lead them to postpone motherhood as they get their careers under way. The postponement can then lead to the eventual decision not to have children at all. According to Harding, many Germans were also not having children due to social reasons, such as inadequate childcare policies.

The number of those with no children has also been on the rise in Italy. In 2002, statistics showed that overall, about 15 percent of Italian women did not have children.[54] The Organisation for Economic Co-operation and Development's figures indicate that 24 percent of women born in 1965 did not have children.[55] Studies like the one conducted by Italian researchers Maria Tanturri and Letizia Mencarini in 2008 showed that 40-44-year-old women with no children tended to be less religious, come from smaller families, and get married a bit later in life. Like the ESRC survey, they also found that women in this age range ended up with no children as an "unintended outcome"—they may have wanted children, but they ended up not having them due to situational factors in their lives.[56]

By 2010, the numbers in Italy jumped to *over 50 percent* of families having no children, and for well over half of them, this was by choice. According to Hilary White of LifeSiteNews.com, 57 percent of "childless households" said they had no children out of "personal choice." The reasons "include a general sense of uncertainty about the future and the inherent difficulties involved in raising children."[57]

In the U.K., a report from the University of Oxford indicates that in 2002, about 21 percent of U.K. women born in 1960 had no children.[58] By 2008, researchers Dylan Kneale and Heather Joshi reported a rise of one in four women and one in five men aged 45 not having children.[59] Recent figures from the Organisation for Economic Co-operation and Development also show a similar rise in U.K. women; of those born around 1965, 19 percent did not have children.[60]

The University of Oxford report also has numbers for additional European countries. In 2002, 18 percent of Finnish women born in 1960 had no children. Similarly, the Organisation for Economic Cooperation and Development numbers indicate that for Finnish women born around 1965, 20 percent did not have children. In the Netherlands, 2002 figures show that 17 percent of women born in 1960 had no children. For those born around 1965, this figure was 18 percent. In Ireland, 2002 data show that 15 percent of women born in 1960 had no children. Recent figures for Irish women born around 1965 are at 18 percent. In Australia, recent figures show that about 16 percent of women born in 1965 did not have children. In Japan, Toshihiko Hara's 2008 study indicates that 13 percent of women born in 1960 had no children. She predicted that the numbers would rise dramatically to 30 percent for those born in 1970. While there is a trend across countries showing that those women who have no children are more highly educated, this does not seem to be as true in Japan.[61 62 63]

Looking at other countries, Kevin Kinsella, formerly of the National Institute on Aging, points us toward East Asia. As economies grow, and more women enter the labor force, he expects fertility rates to drop. Take India, for example, where we are starting to see an uptick of people deciding not to have children. In 2005-06, the Institute for Population Studies found that two percent of women across the country did not have children and did not plan on having them. As Sulabha Parsuraman, Head of the Department of Population Policies and Programs in India, says, "It is a small number. But we are seeing couples making a conscious decision not to have children." As journalists Hemali Chhapia and Malathy Iyer discuss in *The Times of India*, the childless couple is becoming less of a rarity. The times when a couple didn't have a kid meant that friends and family were sure there was "some problem." "Not anymore," they say. "In the new India, people are childless by choice. And the stigma attached to the concept is slowly wearing off."[64] There is also a growing number of men and women in China who are deciding they don't want children. *Los Angeles Times* journalist David Pierson explains that "Economic and social pressures are loosening the filial obligations that have long bound Chinese society." From China to many other countries internationally, parenthood is starting to be seen more as a choice.[65]

NOTES

Chapter 1: Awakening to Pronatalism

1. Lisa Hymas, "2010: The Year the Childfree Went Mainstream (thanks, Oprah!)," *Grist*, December 31, 2010, http://www.grist.org/childfree/2010-12-31-2010-the-year-childfree-went-mainstream-thanks-oprah, accessed December 2010.

2. Ellen Peck and Judith Senderowitz, *Pronatalism: The Myth of Mom & Apple Pie* (New York: Thomas Y. Cromwell Company, 1974), 2.

3. Leslie Lafayette, *Why Don't You Have Kids?* (New York: Zebra Publishing, 1995): Introduction.

4. Ellen L. Walker, *Complete Without Kids* (Austin: Greenleaf Book Group, 2011), 174.

5. Peck and Senderowitz, *Pronatalism*, 1.

6. Allan Carlson, Ph.D, "Marriage and Procreation: On Children as the First Purpose of Marriage," lecture given to the Family Research Council, Washington, DC, on October 20, 2004, adapted in *The Family in America* 18, no. 12 (December 2004), http://www.profam.org/pub/fia/fia_1812.htm, accessed February 2011.

7. Ellen Peck and William Granzig, *The Parent Test: How to Measure and Develop Your Talent for Parenthood* (New York: GP Putnam's Sons, 1978), 30.

8. Ibid.

9. Peck and Senderowitz, *Pronatalism*, 19-28.

10. U.S. Census Bureau, "Fertility of American Women: 2008," under "Population Characteristics," prepared by Jane Lawler Dye (November 2010), http://www.census.gov/prod/2010pubs/p20-563.pdf, accessed January 2011.

11. Anamaria Wilson, "Baby Blues," *Harper's Bazaar*, April 6, 2009, http://www.seattlepi.com/lifestyle/article/Harper-s-Bazaar-Baby-blues-1303132.php, accessed April 2009.

12. Jennifer Senior, "All Joy and No Fun: Why Parents Hate Parenting," under "Features," *New York Times Magazine*, July 4, 2010, 2, http://nymag.com/news/features/67024/, accessed July 2011.

13. Jeremy Adam Smith, "Paid Family Leave's Secret Weapon: Men," *San Francisco Chronicle*, February 3, 2011, http://www.sfgate.com/cgi-bin/article.cgi?f=/c/a/2011/02/03/EDTT1HGM91.DTL, accessed February 2011.

14. Ibid.

15. Pew Research Center, "U.S. Religious Landscape Survey," under "The Pew Forum on Religion and Public Life," http://religions.pewforum.org/reports, accessed June 2011.

16. Peck and Senderowitz, *Pronatalism*, 98-113.

17. Eve Kushner, "Go Forth and Multiply," *Bitch Magazine*, April 2009, http://bitchmagazine.org/article/go-forth-and-multiply, accessed June 2011.

18. Lori Bradley, "Book Review: Finding Childfree Friendly Fiction," *Bella Online*, http://www.bellaonline.com/articles/art44457.asp, accessed November 2010.

19. Gail Collins, *When Everything Changed: The Amazing Journey of American Women from 1960 to the Present* (New York: Back Bay Books, 2010), 351-374.

20. Martin O'Connell, telephone interview by author, April 7, 2010.

Chapter 2: The Destiny Assumption

1. Wikipedia, "Instinct," http://en.wikipedia.org/wiki/Instinct, accessed March 2011.

2. Ellen Peck and Judith Senderowitz, *Pronatalism: The Myth of Mom & Apple Pie* (New York: Thomas Y. Cromwell Company, 1974), 137.

3. Tara Parker-Pope, "Maternal Instinct Is Wired into the Brain," *Well* (blog), *New York Times*, March 7, 2008, http://well.blogs.nytimes.com/2008/03/07/maternal-instinct-is-wired-into-the-brain/, accessed March 2011.

4. Louann Brizendine, *The Female Brain* (New York: Morgan Road Books, 2006), 97.

5. "Why the Biological Clock is Ticking," *Adelaide Now*, January 26, 2010, http://www.adelaidenow.com.au/news/south-australia/why-the-biological-clock-is-ticking/story-e6frea83-1225824115803, accessed March 2011.

6. Betty Rollin, "Motherhood: Who Needs It?" *Look Magazine*, Sept. 22, 1970, http://jackiewhiting.net/collab/exploratory/motherhood.htm, accessed March 2011.

7. Daniel Heimpel, "For Whom the Clock Ticks," *Newsweek*, April 21, 2009, http://www.thedailybeast.com/newsweek/2009/04/21/for-whom-the-clock-ticks.html, accessed March 2011.

8. Concerned Heart, "Turns Out It's Not Just Women Who Have a Biological Clock" *The Male Biological Clock Blogspot* (blog), November 22, 2009, http://themalebiologicalclock.blogspot.

com/2009/11/turns-out-that-its-not-just-women-who.html, accessed March 2011.

9. Harry Fisch, *The Male Biological Clock: The Startling News About Aging, Sexuality, and Fertility in Men* (New York: Free Press, 2004)

10. Peck and Senderowitz, *Pronatalism*, 19-28.

11. "Generation X: Overlooked and Hugely Important Finds New Study from the Center for Work-Life Policy," Center for Work-Life press release, September 16, 2011, on Work Life Policy website, https://www.worklifepolicy.org/documents/X%20Factor%20 Press%20Release%20final.pdf, accessed September 2011.

12. Robert Walker, "Global Population Is Still a Problem," *The Guardian*, July 13, 2010, http://www.guardian.co.uk/environ-ment/2010/jul/13/population-reproduction, accessed March 2011.

13. Abigail Pesta, "To Breed or Not to Breed," *Marie Claire*, September 21, 2009, http://www.marieclaire.com/sex-love/relation-ship-issues/childfree-by-choice?click=main_sr, accessed December 2010.

14. Susan Jeffers, Ph.D., *I'm Okay, You're a Brat!: Setting the Priorities Straight and Freeing You From the Guilt and Mad Myths of Parenthood* (New York: St. Martin's Press, 2001), 153-178.

Chapter 3: The Normality Assumption

1. Michael Cook, "What Is the Ideal Number of Parents? 2? 4? 5?" *Bio Edge*, October 16, 2011, http://www.bioedge.org/index.php/ bioethics/bioethics_article/9785, accessed December 2011.

2. Liz Thomas, "Save the Planet by Having Fewer Babies, Says BBC Presenter as He Calls for Tax Breaks for Small Families," *Daily Mail*, April 5, 2011, http://www.dailymail.co.uk/news/article-

1373368/BBC-presenter-Chris-Packham-says-save-planet-fewer-babies.html, accessed April 2011.

3. Mardy Ireland, *Reconceiving Women: Separating Motherhood from Female Identity* (New York: Guildford Press, 1993), 6.

4. Naomi Rockler-Gladen, "Third Wave Feminism: Personal Empowerment Dominates This Feminist Philosophy," *Suite101*, May 3, 2007, http://www.suite101.com/content/third-wave-feminism-a20276, accessed April 2011.

5. Ireland, *Reconceiving Women*, 91.

6. Cordelia Fine, *Delusions of Gender: How Our Minds, Society, and Neurosexism Create Difference* (New York: W.W. Norton & Company, Inc., 2010), xxvii.

7. Ibid., 25.

8. Mardy Ireland, *Reconceiving Women*, 155.

Chapter 4 : The Marriage Assumption

1. Biography Base, "Augustus Caesar Biography," http://www.biographybase.com/biography/Caesar_Augustus.html, accessed June 2010.

2. Allan Carlson, Ph.D., "Marriage and Procreation: On Children as the First Purpose of Marriage," lecture given to the Family Research Council, Washington, DC, on October 20, 2004, adapted in *The Family in America* 18, no. 12 (December 2004), http://www.profam.org/pub/fia/fia_1812.htm, accessed June 2010.

3. Ibid.

4. Ibid.

5. Ibid.

6. Robert Obach, *Catholic Church on Marital Intercourse: From St. Paul to John Paul II* (United Kingdom: Lexington Books, 2009), 74.

7. John A. Hardon, S.J., "Christian Marriage," in *Moral Theology* (The Real Presence Association, 2004), http://www.therealpresence. org/archives/Moral_Theology/Moral_Theology_006.htm, accessed May 2011.

8. Elaine Tyler May, *Barren in the Promised Land: Childless Americans and the Pursuit of Happiness*, (New York: Basic Books, 1995), 31.

9. Barbara Dafoe Whitehead and David Popenoe, "Life Without Children: The Social Retreat from Children and How It Is Changing America," under Special Reports, *The National Marriage Project*, 39, http://www.virginia.edu/marriageproject/ pdfs/2008LifeWithoutChildren.pdf, accessed May 2011.

10. Ibid.

11. Rosemary Bachelor, "First Birth Control Laws Tied to Promiscuity," *Suite101*, February 13, 2010, http://rosemary-e-bachelor. suite101.com/first-birth-control-laws-tied-to-promiscuity-a201621, accessed June 2011.

12. Carlson, "Marriage and Procreation."

13. United States v. One Package, 86 F. 2d, 737 (1936), http:// www.enotes.com/american-court-cases/united-states-v-one-package, accessed May 2011.

14. Evan Wolfson, *Why Marriage Matters: America, Equality and Gay People's Right to Marry* (New York: Simon and Schuster, 2005), 79.

15. Wikipedia, "Eisenstadt v. Baird," http://en.wikipedia.org/ wiki/Eisenstadt_v._Baird, accessed May, 2011.

16. Carlson, "Marriage and Procreation."

17. Psychology Today Staff, "Marriage, A History," *Psychology Today*, May 1, 2005, http://www.psychologytoday.com/articles/200505/marriage-history, accessed May 2011.

18. Kenneth Magnuson, "Marriage, Procreation & Infertility: Reflections on Genesis," adaptation of a chapter from doctoral dissertation, "Procreation and Childlessness in Theological Perspective: An Examination of the Debate About Reproductive Technology," University of Cambridge, 1997, http://www.sbts.edu/media/publications/sbjt/sbjt_2000spring4.pdf, accessed May 2011.

19. Ibid.

20. Ibid.

21. Ibid.

22. "As Marriage and Parenthood Drift Apart, Public Is Concerned about Social Impact: Generation Gap in Values, Behaviors," Pew Research Center Publications, under "Marriage and Parenthood," July 1, 2007, http://pewresearch.org/pubs/526/marriage-parenthood, accessed May 2011.

23. Ibid.

Chapter 5: The Right to Reproduce Assumption

1. Joanna Nairn, "Is There a Right to Have Children? Substantive Due Process and Probation Conditions that Restrict Reproductive Rights," *Stanford Journal of Civil Rights & Civil Liberties*, Issue 1, 2010, http://lsrj.org/documents/Nairn_Right_To_Have_Children.pdf, accessed June 2011.

2. U.S. Constitution.net, under "Life, Liberty, and the Pursuit of Happiness," http://www.usconstitution.net/constnot.html#life, accessed June 2011.

3. Nairn, Is There a Right to Have Children?, 33.

4. Guttmacher Institute, "Facts on American Teens' Sexual and Reproductive Health," under "Fact Sheets," January 2011, http://www.guttmacher.org/pubs/FB-ATSRH.html, accessed June 2011.

5. Health Teacher, "Child Abuse," http://www.healthteacher.com/content/id/38/, accessed June 2011.

6. Tommy De Seno, "What Do You Think of a Country that Allows You to Abandon Your Child with No Consequence?" *Ricochet*, June 21, 2011, http://ricochet.com/main-feed/What-Do-You-Think-Of-A-Country-That-Allows-You-To-Abandon-Your-Child-With-No-Consequence, accessed June 2011.

7. U.S. Department of Health and Human Services, Child Welfare Information Gateway Foster Care Statistics 2009, May 2011, http://www.childwelfare.gov/pubs/factsheets/foster.pdf#page=1, accessed June 2011.

8. Charles Montaldo, "Women Who Kill Their Children: 11 Women Are on Death Row for Killing Their Kids," About, http://crime.about.com/od/female_offenders/a/mother_killers.htm, accessed June 2011.

9. Save Abandoned Babies Foundation, "Frequently Asked Questions," http://www.saveabandonedbabies.org/resources/FAQ/index.html#, accessed June 2011.

10. Health Teacher, "Child Abuse."

11. The National Campaign to Prevent Teen and Unplanned Pregnancy, "Counting It Up: The Public Costs of Teen Childbearing," http://www.thenationalcampaign.org/costs/, accessed June 2011.

12. Ching-Tung Wang, Ph.D. and John Holton, Ph.D., "Total Estimated Cost of Child Abuse and Neglect in the United States,"

Prevent Child Abuse America, September 2007, http://www.pre-ventchildabuse.org/about_us/media_releases/pcaa_pew_economic_impact_study_final.pdf, accessed June 2011.

13. Pew Charitable Trusts, "Child Abuse and Neglect Cost Nation over $100 Billion per Year," January 29, 2008, http://www.pewtrusts.org/news_room_detail.aspx?id=34676, accessed June 2011.

14. Dustin, "The Cost of Dead-Beat Dads on a Federal Budget," *Our Dime* (blog), July 15, 2010, http://www.ourdime.us/72/bud-getinfo/the-cost-of-dead-beat-dads-on-the-federal-budget/, accessed June 2011.

15. Keli Goff, "Should Fewer Americans Head to College and More Head to Parenting Classes?" *Politics* (blog), *Huffington Post*, June 21, 2011, http://www.huffingtonpost.com/keli-goff/should-less-americans-hea_b_881197.html, accessed June 2011.

16. Ellen Peck and William Granzig, *The Parent Test: How to Measure and Develop Your Talent for Parenthood* (New York: GP Putnam's Sons), 20.

17. Greg Abbott, "Parenting and Paternity Awareness (p.a.p.a.)," under "Child Support," https://www.oag.state.tx.us/cs/ofi/papa/#is, accessed June 2011.

18. Jasmeet Braich, "Parenting Classes Learn About Being Mothers, Fathers," *The Herald*, May 12, 2011, http://www.harber-herald.com/features/2011/05/12/parenting-classes-learn-about-being-mothers-fathers/, accessed June 2011.

19. Richard Garner, "Schools Urged to Teach Good Parenting Skills," *The Independent*, February 2, 2009, http://www.indepen-dent.co.uk/news/education/education-news/schools-urged-to-teach-good-parenting-skills-1522977.html, accessed June 2011.

20. Families Help, http://www.familieshelp.net/, accessed June 2011.

21. Thomas Watkins, "Parents of Los Angeles Gang Kids Head to Class at Court's Order," *Education* (blog), *Huffington Post*, December 12, 2010, http://www.huffingtonpost.com/2010/12/12/los-angeles-gang-parents-_n_795620.html, accessed June 2011.

22. Peck and Granzig, *The Parent Test*, 24.

23. Ibid., 23.

24. Ibid., 27.

25. Ibid., 28.

26. Ibid., 34.

27. Ibid., 35.

28. Evan Ackerman, "Radical New Birth Control for Men: 100% Effective for 10 Years," *Dv!ce*, May 31, 2011, http://dvice.com/archives/2011/05/injectable-birt.php, accessed June 2011.

29. Mimi Zieman, MD, "Patient Information: Long term Methods of Birth Control," Up to Date, September 11, 2011, http://www.uptodate.com/contents/patient-information-long-term-methods-of-birth-control-beyond-the-basics, accessed September 2011.

Chapter 6: The Offspring Assumption

1. Data excerpted from Lisa Hymas, "I am the Population Problem," *RH Reality Check*, August 25, 2011, Chart, http://www.rhrealitycheck.org/blog/2011/08/16/i-population-problem-0, accessed August 2011.

2. Vicky Markham, "By the Numbers: Population, Consumption, and Reproductive Health," *RH Reality Check*, August 17,

2011, http://www.rhrealitycheck.org/blog/2011/08/16/numbers-population-consumption-reproductive-health, accessed August 2011.

3. Hymas, "I am the Population Problem."

4. Long Fence and Home, "What is Your Impact on the Environment?" under "Carbon Footprint," http://www.longfenceandhome.com/les/carbon-footprint/ accessed July 2011.

5. Simon Rogers and Lisa Evans, "World Carbon Dioxide Emissions Data by Country: China Speeds Ahead of the Rest," *Datablog* (blog), *The Guardian*, January 31, 2011, http://www.guardian.co.uk/news/datablog/2011/jan/31/world-carbon-dioxide-emissions-country-data-co2, accessed July 2011.

6. Markham, "By the Numbers."

7. Hymas, "I am the Population Problem."

8. Paul A. Murtaugh and Michael G. Schlax, "Reproduction and the Carbon Legacies of Individuals," *Global Environmental Change* 19 (October 2008): 14-20, http://blog.oregonlive.com/environment_impact/2009/07/carbon%20legacy.pdf, accessed August 2011.

9. World Business Council for Sustainable Development, "Responding to the Biodiversity Challenge," report summary, http://www.wbcsd.org/Pages/EDocument/EDocumentDetails.aspx?ID=22&NoSearchContextKey=true, accessed January 2012.

10. World Population Balance, "Current Population is Three Times the Sustainable Level," http://www.worldpopulationbalance.org/3_times_sustainable, accessed August 2011.

11. David Paxson, telephone interview by author, August 26, 2011, with special reference to Global Footprint Network, "Data

and Results," http://www.footprintnetwork.org/en/index.php/GFN/page/ecological_footprint_atlas_2008.

12. World Population Balance, "Current Population is Three Times the Sustainable Level."

13. Paxson telephone interview.

14. World Population Balance, "Current Population is Three Times the Sustainable Level."

15. World Population Balance, "Current Population is 3x Sustainable Level," *Balanced View*, August 2007, http://www.world-populationbalance.org/wpb_newsletters/wpb_newsletter_2007aug.pdf, accessed August 2011.

16. World Population Balance, "World Population Balance Boards and Staff," http://www.worldpopulationbalance.org/boards_and_staff, accessed August 2011.

17. "Family Planning: A Major Environmental Emphasis," Oregon State University news & research communications release, July 31, 2009, Oregon State University website, http://oregonstate.edu/ua/ncs/archives/2009/jul/family-planning-major-environmental-emphasis, accessed August 2011.

18. CNN, "The Cafferty File: Overpopulation and the Earth's Limited Natural Resources," YouTube, http://www.youtube.com/watch?v=LlcJoZyG2N4, accessed July 2011.

19. Bill McKibben, *Maybe One* (New York: Plume, 1999), 10.

20. Ibid.

21. Lauren Sandler, "The Only Child: Debunking the Myths," *TIME*, July 8, 2010, http://www.time.com/time/magazine/article/0,9171,2002530-2,00.html, accessed July 2010.

22. Dina McQueen, "Overpopulation, the Environment and Adoption: An Urgent Call to Action," *Green* (blog), *Huffington Post*, September 1, 2011, http://www.huffingtonpost.com/dina-mcqueen/overpopulation-adoption_b_943436.html?ir=Green, accessed September 2011.

23. Hope for Orphans, "Four Myths of Adoption," under "Adoption," http://www.hopefororphans.org/Display.asp?Page=fourmyths, accessed September 2011.

24. Mardie Caldwell, COAP, "6 Common Adoption Myths Dispelled," MSNBC *Today*, under "Parenting," May 9, 2007, http://today.msnbc.msn.com/id/18557471/ns/today-parenting/t/common-adoption-myths-dispelled/, accessed July 2011.

25. Hope for Orphans, "Four Myths of Adoption."

26. Caldwell, "6 Common Adoption Myths Dispelled."

27. Hope for Orphans, "Four Myths of Adoption."

28. Caldwell, "6 Common Adoption Myths Dispelled."

29. Hope for Orphans, "Four Myths of Adoption."

30. Caldwell, "6 Common Adoption Myths Dispelled."

31. Paxson telephone interview.

32. Carbon Tax Center, "About," http://www.carbontax.org/about/, accessed August 2011.

33. Paxson telephone interview.

Chapter 7: The Fulfillment Assumption

1. Ellen Peck and Judith Senderowitz, *Pronatalism: The Myth of Mom & Apple Pie* (New York: Thomas Y. Cromwell Company, 1974), 19-28.

2. Nancy Hass, "Time to Chill? Egg-freezing Technology Offers Women a Chance to Extend Their Fertility," *Vogue*, April 28, 2011, http://www.vogue.com/magazine/article/time-to-chill-egg-freezing-technology-offers-a-chance-to-extend-fertility/, accessed September 2011.

3. Ibid.

4. Rufus Griscom and Alisa Volkman, "Let's Talk Parenting Taboos," *Ted*, under "Talks," December 2010, http://www.ted.com/talks/rufus_griscom_alisa_volkman_let_s_talk_parenting_taboos.html, accessed September 2011.

5. Wray Herbert, "The Myth of Joyful Parenthood: The Ultimate Cognitive Dissonance?" *Healthy Living* (blog), *Huffington Post*, February 2, 2011, http://www.huffingtonpost.com/wray-herbert/joyful-parenthood-myth-cognitive-dissonance_b_816453.html, accessed September 2011.

6. Richard P. Eibach and Steven E. Mock, "Idealizing Parenthood to Rationalize Parental Investments," abstract, *Psychological Science 22*, no.2 (January 18, 2011): 203-08, http://pss.sagepub.com/content/early/2011/01/18/0956797610397057.abstract, accessed September 2011.

7. Abigail Pesta, "To Breed or Not to Breed?" *Marie Claire*, September 21, 2009, http://www.marieclaire.com/sex-love/relationship-issues/childfree-by-choice, accessed September 2009.

8. Lisa Belkin, "A Father with Regrets," *Motherlode: Adventures in Parenting* (blog), *New York Times*, June 10, 2011, http://parenting.blogs.nytimes.com/2011/06/10/a-father-with-regrets/, accessed September 2011.

9. Fallyn, June 19, 2011 (11:53 a.m.), comment on Laura Carroll, "Getting Real About Regret," *La Vie Childfree: Talk Childfree and Beyond with Laura Carroll* (blog), June 16, 2011, http://

lauracarroll.com/2011/06/getting-real-about-regret/, accessed June 2011.

10. John Hearne, "Parent Trap: Those Growing Pains," Herald. ie, August 5, 2010, http://www.herald.ie/lifestyle/parents/parent-trap-those-growing-pains-2285251.html, accessed September 2011.

11. Jennifer Senior, "All Joy and No Fun: Why Parents Hate Parenting," under "Features," *New York Magazine*, July 4, 2010, http://nymag.com/news/features/67024/, accessed July 2011.

12. Lauren Sandler, "The American Nightmare: We Have Everything the American Dream Prescribed. So Why Aren't We Happy?" *Psychology Today*, March 15, 2011, http://www.psychologytoday.com/articles/201103/the-american-nightmare, accessed April 2011.

13. Senior, "All Joy and No Fun."

14. Sandler, "The American Nightmare."

15. Laura Carroll, *Finding Fulfillment from the Inside Out* (AuthorHouse, 2000), 53-69.

Chapter 8: The Elderhood Assumption

1. U.S. Census Bureau, "U.S. & World Population Clocks," http://www.census.gov/main/www/popclock.html, accessed October 2011.

2. U.S. Census Bureau, "State and County Quick Facts," http://quickfacts.census.gov/qfd/states/00000.html, accessed October 2011.

3. Adele M. Hayutin, Ph.D, Miranda Dietz and Lillian Mitchell, "New Realities of an Older America: Challenges, Changes, and Questions," Stanford Center on Longevity, 2010, 41, http://longevity.stanford.edu/files2/New%20Realities%20of%20an%20Older%20America_0.pdf accessed October 2011.

4. Federal Interagency Forum on Aging-Related Statistics, "Older Americans 2010: Keys Indicators of Well Being," July 2010, 8, http://www.agingstats.gov/agingstatsdotnet/Main_Site/Data/2010_Documents/Docs/OA_2010.pdf, accessed October 2011.

5. Elena Portacolone, "The Myth of Independence for Older Americans Living Alone in the Bay Area of San Francisco: A Critical Reflection," *Aging & Society* 31, no. 5 (July 2011): 803–28.

6. McKnight's Long Term Care News & Assisted Living, "How Many Assisted Living Facilities Exist?" January 1, 2008, http://www.mcknights.com/how-many-assisted-living-facilities-exist/article/104028/, accessed October 2011.

7. Bill Thomas, "Learn to Value Life in Elderhood," *San Francisco Chronicle*, June 3, 2011, http://www.sfgate.com/cgi-bin/article.cgi?f=/c/a/2011/06/03/EDMM1JOKCO.DTL, accessed June 2011.

8. Federal Interagency Forum on Aging-Related Statistics Report, "Older Americans 2010: Keys Indicators of Well Being," xv, 20.

9. Sandra Block, "Elder Care Shifting Away from Nursing Homes," ABC, under "News/Money," February 2, 2008, http://abcnews.go.com/Business/story?id=4230852&page=1, accessed October 2011.

10. Ibid.

11. Laura Carroll, *Families of Two: Interviews with Happily Married Couples Without Children by Choice* (Xlibris Press, 2000), 29.

12. Elena Portacolone, telephone interview by author, June 1, 2011.

13. Walecia Konrad, "Taking Care of Parents Also Means Taking Care of Finances," *New York Times*, September 18, 2009, http://

www.nytimes.com/2009/09/19/health/19patient.html?ref=health, accessed October 2011.

14. "Washington Week," PBS, June 3, 2011.

15. Sam Ali, "Help Employees Care for Parents," Diversity Inc., September 27, 2010, http://www.agedcommunity.asn.au/mature-workers-matter/downloads/resources/flexible-work-practices/Help%20Employees%20Care%20for%20Parents.pdf, accessed December 2011.

16. Eamonn Duff, "Why Old Souls are Abandoned," *Sydney Morning Herald*, May 22, 2011, http://www.smh.com.au/national/why-old-souls-are-abandoned-20110521-1exnv.html, accessed October 2011.

17. U.S. Census Bureau, Tavia Simmons and Jane Lawler Dye, "Grandparents Living with Grandchildren: 2000," *Census 2000 Brief*, October 2003, http://www.census.gov/prod/2003pubs/c2kbr-31.pdf, accessed October 2011.

18. Alicia Marie Belchak, "In Old Age, Childless Adults Just as Content as Parents," Yahoo News, under "Health," December 15, 2000, accessed December 2000.

19. Portacolone telephone interview.

20. Carroll, *Families of Two*, 123.

21. Thomas, "Learn to Value Life in Elderhood."

22. Portacolone, "The Myth of Independence."

23. Pearl Dykstra and Gunhild Hagestad, "Roads Less Taken: Developing a Nuanced View of Older Adults Without Children," *Journal of Family Issues* 28, no. 10 (October 2007): 1275-1310, and Z. Zhang and M. D. Hayward, "Childlessness and Psychological Well-Being of Older Persons," in "Series B: Psychological Sciences

and Social Sciences," *Journals of Gerontology* 56, S5 (September 2001), http://jfi.sagepub.com/content/28/10/1275.abstract, http://www.ncbi.nlm.nih.gov/pubmed/11522813: S311-S320, accessed January 2011.

24. Portacolone telephone interview.

25. Ibid.

26. Portacolone, "The Myth of Independence."

Chapter 9: The Transition Has Already Begun

1. Martin O'Connell, telephone interview by author, April 7, 2010.

2. U.S. Census Bureau, "Fertility of American Women: 2008," prepared by Jane Lawler Dye (November 2010), http://www.census.gov/prod/2010pubs/p20-563.pdf, accessed January 2011.

3. Gretchen Livingston and D'Vera Cohn, "More Women Without Children," Pew Research Center, under "Pew Social and Demographic Trends," June 25, 2010, http://pewresearch.org/pubs/1642/more-women-without-children, accessed July 2010.

4. Brian Alexander, "Marriage Eludes High-Achieving Black Women," MSNBC, August 13, 2009, http://www.msnbc.msn.com/id/32379727/ns/health-sexual_health/t/marriage-eludes-high-achieving-black-women/#.TuOw3lbNmCc, accessed January 2011.

5. Nadra Kareem Nittle, "The Media Thinks Single Black Women Have All the Problems," Change.org, June 29, 2010, http://news.change.org/stories/the-media-thinks-single-black-women-have-all-the-problems, accessed January 2011.

6. Livingston and Cohn, "More Women Without Children."

7. Ibid.

8. Ibid.

9. Dye, "Fertility of American Women."

10. "The Census Bureau Reports 'Delayer Boom' as More Educated Women Have Children Later," U.S. Census Bureau press release, May 9, 2011, U.S. Census Bureau website, http://www.census.gov/newsroom/releases/archives/fertility/cb11-83.html, accessed May 2011.

11. Livingston and Cohn, "More Women Without Children."

12. "Generation X: Overlooked and Hugely Important Finds New Study from the Center for Work-Life Policy," X Factor press release, September 16, 2011, https://www.worklifepolicy.org/documents/X%20Factor%20Press%20Release%20final.pdf, accessed September 2011.

Chapter 10: Toward a Post-Pronatal Society

1. Bruce Chernof and Steven P. Wallace, "How the Bay Area Can Afford Old Age," under "Open Forum," *San Francisco Chronicle*, September 16, 2011, http://www.sfgate.com/cgi-bin/article.cgi?f=/c/a/2011/09/16/EDQD1L44TR.DTL, accessed September 2011.

2. Katherine Bindley, "Gen X Women Succeed at Work, Have Fewer Kids: Study," *Women* (blog), *Huffington Post*, September 13, 2011, http://www.huffingtonpost.com/2011/09/13/gen-x-study_n_959256.html?ref=mostpopular, accessed September 2011.

3. Ibid.

4. Elinor Burkett, *The Baby Boon: How Family-Friendly America Cheats the Childless* (New York: The Free Press, 2000), Amazon.com review, http://www.amazon.com/

Baby-Boon-Family-Friendly-America-Childless/dp/0743242645/ref
=sr_1_1?ie=UTF8&qid=1328665252&sr=8-1, accessed February
2011.

5. Sky Scanner, "Tips and Advice," under "Family
Travel," August 23, 2010, http://www.skyscanner.net/news/
articles/2010/08/007776-59-of-travellers-want-family-only-section-
on-flights.html, accessed October 2010.

6. Ben Mutzabaugh, "New Ryanair Fee Is Real, But What
About Pledge of Child-Free Flights?" *Today in the Sky with Ben
Mutzabaugh* (blog), *USA Today*, March 31, 2011, http://travel.usa-
today.com/flights/post/2011/03/ryanair-child-free-flights/150159/1,
accessed March 2011.

7. Wikipedia, "National Alliance for Optional Parenthood,"
http://en.wikipedia.org/wiki/National_Alliance_for_Optional_Par-
enthood, accessed March 2010.

8. Rockefeller Brothers Fund Inc., Internal NAOP Grant
Proposal, RBE 7S-178, October 1975.

9. John Vidal, "Rich Nations to Offset Emissions with Birth
Control," *The Guardian*, December 3, 2009, http://www.guardian.
co.uk/environment/2009/dec/03/carbon-offset-projects-climate-
change?showallcomments=true, accessed November 2011.

10. Vicky Markham, "By the Numbers: Population, Consumption, and Reproductive Health," *RH Reality Check*, August 17,
2011, http://www.rhrealitycheck.org/blog/2011/08/16/numbers-
population-consumption-reproductive-health, accessed September
2011.

Appendix

1. Martin O'Connell, telephone interview by author, April 7,
2010.

2. U.S. Census Bureau, "Fertility of American Women: June 2000," prepared by Amara Bachu and Martin O'Connell, http://www.census.gov/prod/2001pubs/p20-543rv.pdf, accessed December 2010.

3. Census figures obtained in 2000 from 1998 census data tables.

4. Stuart Basten, Ph.D, "Voluntary Childlessness and Being Childfree," *The Future of Human Reproduction*, Working Paper No. 5, 2009, http://www.sjc.ox.ac.uk/3155/WP48%20Voluntary%20childlessness%20and%20being%20childfree1.pdf.download, accessed December 2010.

5. Author, based on data collected as part of interview research, 1999.

6. Pearl Dykstra and Gunhild Hagestad, "Roads Less Taken: Developing a Nuanced View of Older Adults Without Children," *Journal of Family Issues* 1275, no. 28 (2007).

7. Gunhild Hagestad and Vaughn R.A. Call, "Pathways to Childlessness: A Life Course Perspective," abstract, *Journal of Family Issues* 1338, no. 28 (October 2007): 1338-1361.

8. Alicia Marie Belchak, "In Old Age, Childless Adults Just as Content as Parents," Yahoo News, under "Health," December 15, 2000, accessed December 2000.

9. J. Cwikel, H. Gramotnev, and C. Lee, (2006). "Never Married Childless Women in Australia: Health and Social Circumstances in Older Age," *Social Science and Medicine* 62, no. 8 (2006): 1991-2001.

10. Gunhild Hagestad and Vaughn R.A. Call, "Pathways to Childlessness," abstract.

11. Z. Zhang and M. D. Hayward, "Childlessness and Psychological Well-Being of Older Persons," in "Series B: Psychological

Sciences and Social Sciences," *Journal of Gerontology* 56, S5 (September 2001), http://www.ncbi.nlm.nih.gov/pubmed/11522813: S311-S320, accessed December 2010.

12. Regina M. Bures, Tanya Koropeckyj-Cox, and Michael Loree, "Childlessness, Parenthood, and Depressive Symptoms Among Middle-Aged and Older Adults," *Journal of Family Issues* 30, no. 5 (May 2009): 670-687.

13. Robert Plotnick, "Childlessness and Economic Well-Being of Older Americans," in "Series B: Psychological Sciences and Social Sciences," *Journal of Gerontology* 64B, no. 6 (November 2009): 767-776, http://www.ncbi.nlm.nih.gov/pmc/articles/PMC2905129/, accessed January 2011.

14. Sherryl Jeffries and Candace Konnert, "Regret and Psychological Well-Being Among Voluntarily and Involuntarily Childless Women and Mothers," *International Journal of Aging and Human Development* 54, no. 2 (2002): 89-106, http://www.mendeley.com/research/regret-psychological-wellbeing-among-voluntarily-involuntarily-childless-women-mothers/, accessed January 2010.

15. Belchak, "In Old Age."

16. G. Clare Wenger, Pearl A. Dykstra, Tuula Melkas, and Kees C.P.M. Knipscheer, "Social Embeddedness and Late-Life Parenthood: Community Activity, Close Ties, and Support Networks," *Journal of Family Issues* 28, no. 11 (November 2007): 1419-1456.

17. Pearl Dykstra, "Off the Beaten Track: Childlessness & Social Integration in Late Life," abstract, *Research on Aging* 28, no. 6 (November 2006): 749-767.

18. Emily Grundy, "Women's Fertility and Mortality in Late Mid Life: A Comparison of Three Contemporary Populations," *American Journal of Human Biology* 21, no. 4 (July/August 2009): 541–547.

19. Gunilla Ringbäck Weitoft, Bo Burström, and Måns Rosén, "Premature Mortality Among Lone Fathers and Childless Men," *Social Science & Medicine* 59, no. 7 (2004): 1449-1459, http://www.ncbi.nlm.nih.gov/pubmed/15246173, accessed January 2011.

20. Basten, "Voluntary Childlessness and Being Childfree," 10.

21. Kristin Park, "Choosing Childlessness: Weber's Typology of Action and Motives of the Voluntary Childless," *Sociological Inquiry* 75, no. 3 (August 2005): 372-402.

22. Yve Stöbel-Richter, Manfred E. Beutel, Carolyn Finck, and Elmar Brähler, "The 'Wish to Have a Child,' Childlessness and Infertility in Germany," *Human Reproduction* 20, no. 10 (October 2005): 2850-57.

23. Renske Keizer, Pearl A. Dysktra, and Miranda D. Jansen, "Pathways into Childlessness: Evidence of Gendered Life Course Dynamics," *Journal of Biosocial Science* 40, no. 6 (December 2007): 863-78.

24. Ariene Kemkes Grottenthaler, "Postponing or Rejecting Parenthood? Results of a Survey Among Female Academic Professionals," *Journal of Biosocial Science* 35, no. 2 (2003): 213–26.

25. Dylan Kneale and Heather Joshi, "Postponement and Childlessness: Evidence from Two British Cohorts," *Demographic Research* 19, no. 58 (November 2008): 1935-64.

26. Kristin Park, "Stigma Management Among the Voluntary Childless," *Sociological Perspectives* 45, no. 1 (Spring 2002): 21-45.

27. Laurie Chancey and Susan A. Dumais, "Voluntary Childlessness in Marriage and Family Textbooks, 1950-2000," *Journal of Family History* 34, no. 2 (2009): 206-33.

28. Letha D. Scanzoni and John H. Scanzoni, *Men, Women, and Change: A Sociology of Marriage and Family* (New York: McGraw-Hill, 1976), 399-400.

29. Chancey and Dumais, "Voluntary Childlessness in Marriage and Family Textbooks."

30. Tanya Koropeckyj-Cox and Gretchen Pendell, "The Gender Gap in Attitudes About Childlessness in the United States," *Journal of Marriage and Family* 69, no. 4 (November 2007): 899-915.

31. Mardy S. Ireland, *Reconceiving Women: Separating Mother-hood from Female Identity* (New York: Guildford Press, 1993), 17-70.

32. Myra J. Hird, "Vacant Wombs: Feminist Challenges to Psychoanalytic Theories of Childless Women," *Feminist Review*, no. 75 (2003): 5-19.

33. Rosemary Gillespie, "When No Means No: Disbelief, Disregard and Deviance as Discourses of Voluntary Childlessness," *Women's Studies International Forum* 23, no. 2 (March-April 2000): 223-34.

34. Christine Brooks, Ph.D. "Being True to Myself: A Grounded Theory Explanation of the Process and Meaning of Early Articulation of Voluntary Childlessness" (doctoral dissertation, Institute of Transpersonal Psychology, 2007), 79.

35. Ibid., 24, 29, 79.

36. Rosemary Balsam, "Integrating Male and Female Elements in a Woman's Gender Identity," *Journal of the American Psychoana-lytic Association* 49, no. 4 (December 2001): 1335-60.

37. Lorraine Ali, "Does Having Kids Make You Happy?" *Newsweek*, June 28, 2008, http://www.newsweek.com/2008/06/28/having-kids-makes-you-happy.html, accessed January 2011.

38. Jean M. Twenge, W. Keith Campbell, and Craig A. Foster, "Parenthood and Marital Satisfaction: A Meta-Analytic Review," *Journal of Marriage and Family* 65, no. 3 (August 2003): 574–83.

39. Ali, "Does Having Kids Make You Happy?"

40. Ibid.

41. Ibid.

42. "State of Our Unions: The Social Health of Marriage in America: 2006," *The National Marriage Project*, no.8 (2006): 12, http://www.virginia.edu/marriageproject/pdfs/SOOU2006.pdf, accessed January 2011.

43. Jennifer Senior, "All Joy and No Fun: Why Parents Hate Parenting," *New York Times Magazine*, July 4, 2010, http://nymag.com/news/features/67024/, accessed July 2011.

44. Today Show, NBC, July 15, 2010.

45. Senior, "All Joy and No Fun," 6.

46. "Childlessness in Europe," Research Report to the Economic and Social Research Council (ESRC) on the Project Funded by Research Grant RES-000-23-0074 (December 2002-July 2003): 1-9, http://www.esrc.ac.uk/my-esrc/grants/RES-000-23-0074/outputs/Read/66c5d0b8-ca7a-4688-949a-423588329820, accessed January 2011.

47. Ibid., 2.

48. U.S. Census Fertility Department, interview by author, fall 2008.

49. Donald Rowland, "Historical Trends in Childlessness," *Journal of Family Issues* 28, no. 10 (October 2007): 1311-37.

50. Toshihiko Hara, "Increasing Childlessness in Germany and Japan: Toward a Childless Society?" *International Journal of Japanese Sociology* 17, no. 1 (December 2008): 42-62.

51. Luke Harding, "Germany Agonizes over 30% Childless Women," *The Guardian*, January 26, 2006, http://www.guardian.co.uk/world/2006/jan/27/germany.lukeharding, accessed January 2011.

52. Daniel Martin, "Barren Britain: 19% of Women Are Childless at Menopause," Mail Online, May 19, 2011, http://www.dailymail.co.uk/news/article-1388477/Barren-Britain-19-women-childless-menopause.html, accessed May 2011.

53. Stöbel-Richter, Beutel, Finck, and Brähler, "The 'Wish to Have a Child,'" 2850-57.

54. Basten, "Voluntary Childlessness and Being Childfree," 3.

55. Martin, "Barren Britain."

56. Maria Letizia Tanturri and Letizia Mencarini, "Childless or Childfree? Paths to Voluntary Childlessness in Italy," *Population and Development Review* 34, no. 1 (March 2008): 51-77.

57. Hilary White, "Over Half of Italian Families Childless: Report," LifeSite News, March 24, 2010, http://www.lifesitenews.com/news/archive/ldn/2010/mar/10032405, accessed January 2011.

58. Basten, "Voluntary Childlessness and Being Childfree," 3.

59. Kneale and Joshi, "Postponement and Childlessness," 1935-68.

60. Martin, "Barren Britain."

61. O'Connell, telephone interview.

62. Martin, "Barren Britain."

63. Gretchen Livingston and D'Vera Cohn, "Childlessness up Among All Women; Down Among Women with Advanced Degrees," Pew Research Center, under "Pew Social and Demographic Trends," June 25, 2010, http://www.pewsocialtrends. org/2010/06/25/childlessness-up-among-all-women-down-among-women-with-advanced-degrees/, accessed June 2010.

64. Hemali Chhapia and Malathy Iyer, "Oh Baby, No Baby!" *Times of India*, September 23, 2010, http://articles.timesofindia. indiatimes.com/2010-09-23/man-woman/28214410_1_monisha-childless-couple-ias-officer, accessed September 2010.

65. David Pierson, "In China, Having Children Is No Longer a Given," *Los Angeles Times*, September 2, 2011, http://articles. latimes.com/2011/sep/02/business/la-fi-china-no-child-20110903, accessed September 2011.

ABOUT THE AUTHOR

Laura Carroll is the author of *Families of Two: Interviews With Happily Married Couples Without Children by Choice*, and *Finding Fulfillment From the Inside Out.*

In addition to writing nonfiction books, she has worked over the last 15 years as a business and litigation psychology consultant and used her expertise in behavioral sciences, psychology, and communications to advise business, legal, and nonprofit professionals on their communications strategies and goals.

Laura is a seasoned leader of personal and professional development seminars, and has appeared on a variety of television shows, including *Good Morning America* and *The Early Show*. She has been a guest on many radio talk shows to discuss childfree and social science topics.

You'll find her online at her nonfiction book site, LiveTrue Books, her top childfree blog, La Vie Childfree, and her consulting site, Carroll Communications.

18153023R00100

Printed in Great Britain
by Amazon